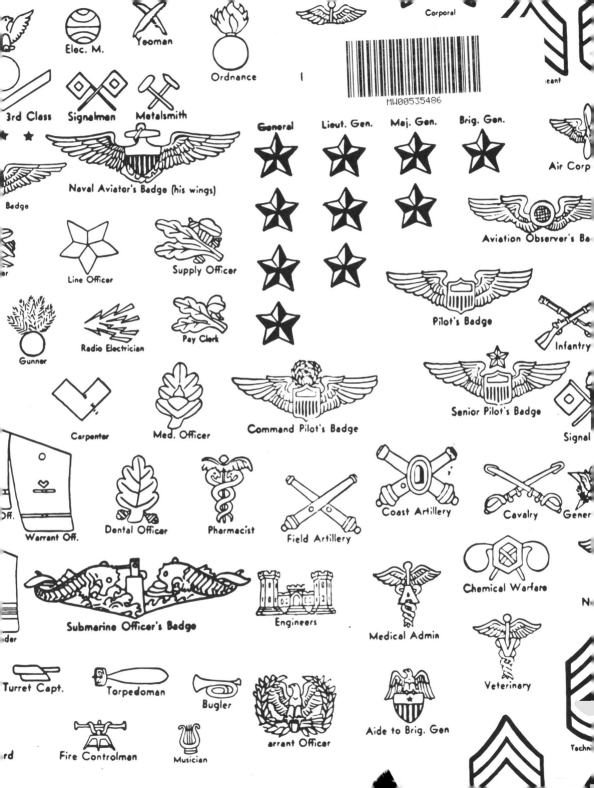

Elec. M.

Yeoman

Corporal

Ordnance

I

3rd Class

Signalman

Metalsmith

General

Lieut. Gen.

Maj. Gen.

Brig. Gen.

Air Corp

Naval Aviator's Badge (his wings)

Badge

Line Officer

Supply Officer

Aviation Observer's Ba

Gunner

Radio Electrician

Pay Clerk

Pilot's Badge

Infantry

Carpenter

Med. Officer

Command Pilot's Badge

Senior Pilot's Badge

Signal

Off.

Warrant Off.

Dental Officer

Pharmacist

Field Artillery

Coast Artillery

Cavalry

Gener

Submarine Officer's Badge

Engineers

Medical Admin

Chemical Warfare

N

der

Turret Capt.

Torpedoman

Bugler

arrant Officer

Aide to Brig. Gen

Veterinary

rd

Fire Controlman

Musician

Technic

MY LIFE
IN THE SERVICE

The World War II Diary of George McGovern

Introduction by Andrew J. Bacevich

FRANKLIN
SQUARE
PRESS

New York

Copyright © 2016 Franklin Square Press

All rights reserved.

Published by Franklin Square Press, a division of *Harper's Magazine*

666 Broadway, 11th Floor, New York, NY 10012

First Edition

First Printing 2016

ISBN: 978-1-879957-59-6

Library of Congress Cataloging-in-Publication Data

Names: McGovern, George S. (George Stanley), 1922-2012, author.
Title: My life in the service : the World War II diary of George McGovern /
introduction by Andrew J. Bacevich.
Other titles: World War II diary of George McGovern
Description: New York : Franklin Square Press, [2016]
Identifiers: LCCN 2016027801 | ISBN 9781879957596 (hardcover)
Subjects: LCSH: McGovern, George S. (George Stanley), 1922-2012--Diaries. |
McGovern, George S. (George Stanley), 1922-2012--Military service. |
Bomber pilots--United States--Biography. | United States. Army Air Forces.
Bombardment Squadron, 741st--Biography. | Bombing,
Aerial--Europe--History--20th century. | World War, 1939-1945--Aerial
operations, American. | World War, 1939-1945--Campaigns--Europe. | World
War, 1939-1945--Personal narratives. | Legislators--United
States--Biography. | United States. Congress. Senate--Biography.
Classification: LCC E840.8.M34 A3 2016 | DDC 973.923092 [B] --dc23
LC record available at https://lccn.loc.gov/2016027801

Printed in Taunton, Massachusetts, United States of America

10 9 8 7 6 5 4 3 2 1

CONTENTS

Before he became a celebrated politician, or even graduated from college, Senator George McGovern served as a B-24 bomber pilot in World War II. Based in Italy, he flew thirty-five combat missions over German-occupied Europe between 1944 and 1945, earning the Distinguished Flying Cross for his ingenuity in the face of adversity.

After the war, McGovern returned to his family and his studies, becoming a professor of history and political science in his native South Dakota. He left academia to enter politics full-time in 1955, beginning his long career by resuscitating the state's Democratic Party.

McGovern was elected to the U.S. House of Representatives in 1956 and 1958, and then to the Senate in 1962, an office he would hold for eighteen years. He was the Democratic nominee for president in 1972.

Over the course of his career, McGovern received special appointments from Presidents Kennedy, Ford, Carter, and Clinton on a range of issues, including global hunger and nuclear disarmament. He was the president of the Middle East Policy Council from 1991 to 1998, became the first United Nations global ambassador on hunger in 2001, and was a *Harper's Magazine* board member from 1990 until his death, in 2012, at the age of ninety.

George McGovern, 1943

INTRODUCTION

By Andrew J. Bacevich

The World War II diary of Lieutenant George McGovern offers an intimate glimpse into an immense undertaking—the Allied bombing of Nazi-occupied Europe. In our day, strategic bombing implies the precise targeting of specific sites thought to possess great value. Back when Lieutenant McGovern flew with the 455th Bombardment Group, dozens or even hundreds of airplanes plastered an area with tons of ordnance in hopes of hitting something useful. In our day, American combat aircraft are very rarely lost to enemy action; during McGovern's war, losing aircraft was simply the cost of doing business. The killing and destruction wrought by Allied bombing occurred on a staggering scale. So too did the losses absorbed by those delivering the bombs.

The 455th Group was part of the 15th Air Force, which initially operated from bases in North Africa but occupied more than twenty airfields in southern Italy by the time McGovern joined his outfit in late 1944. Ranging across southern and central Europe, the 15th Air Force mostly flew the B-24 Liberators, a plane less well known today than the B-17 Flying Fortress immortalized in movies such as *Command Decision* (1948) and *Twelve O'Clock High* (1949). Yet the B-24 flew faster than the B-17 and could carry a larger bomb load farther. In addition, more Liberators rolled out of U.S. aviation plants than any other bomber: more than 18,000 by the time the war ended. By way of comparison, the production run of the U.S. Air Force's current frontline bomber, the B-2 Spirit, ended at twenty-one.

Wartime imperatives expedited design and production. Consolidated Aircraft signed the initial contract to build the four-

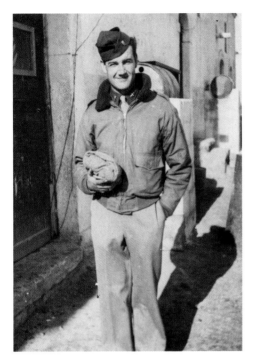

engine B-24 in March 1939. Just two years later, the plane was already coming into service. Firms larger than Consolidated handled most of the actual production. Ford manufactured thousands of Liberators at its huge Willow Run plant near Ypsilanti, Michigan.

The hastily designed B-24 was not without flaws. It was unwieldy, uncomfortable, and, as McGovern himself learned, unreliable. Once fielded, the Liberator experienced a disturbingly high accident rate. In the year after McGovern enlisted, for example, Second Air Force B-24s were involved in more than 290 accidents. In combat, the plane demonstrated a limited capacity to sustain damage. Bailing out of a crippled Liberator posed a challenge—hence, its nickname, the "Flying Coffin."

The mass production of aircraft required the mass production of aircrews. Like Ford at Willow Run, the Army Air Forces applied assembly-line methods, producing 193,000 pilots between 1939 and 1945. These were citizen-warriors, not career professionals. To acquire the skills of a combat aviator, they moved step-by-step through a detailed training regimen before graduating to crew a particular aircraft type. From start to finish, the course of instruction could take a year or more, involving many changes of station. McGovern's vagabond journey took him from South Dakota to Missouri and then on to Illinois, Texas (twice), Oklahoma, Kansas (twice), Nebraska, and finally Idaho—with time out along the way to marry his hometown sweetheart, Eleanor Stegeberg, who soon became pregnant. The training itself was not easy. Around 140,000 candidates washed out of flight school without getting their wings. The twenty-two-year-old McGovern excelled.

When most World War II soldiers, sailors, and Marines shipped out, they did so expecting to remain overseas for the duration of the fighting. For airmen, a different standard applied. Upon completing a set number of combat missions—typically thirty-five—they became eligible to return home. Between each of those missions, moreover, airmen slept in beds and generally enjoyed decent meals. To the average infantryman in a muddy foxhole dining on cold C rations, pilots seemed to have it pretty good. That's the way Bill Mauldin's Willie and Joe saw it, at least.

It was all a matter of perspective. On each combat mission, bomber crews faced extraordinary hazards, most of which McGovern himself encountered. Apart from the shortcomings of the planes, navigation aids and weather forecasting were rudimentary, at least by today's standards. Simply getting to the target area represented something of an achievement. To arrive inevitably meant getting shot at, either by enemy air defenses—"flak," in the parlance of the day—or by Luftwaffe fighters. Then there was the problem of returning to home base, a trip all too often complicated by equipment failures, fuel shortages, or mistakes by crewmen exhausted from the exertions and the occasional terror of eight to ten hours in the air.

As the pilot in command of a B-24, Lieutenant McGovern gained combat experience that was both typical and extraordinary, as readers of this understated account will appreciate. Unlike many of his comrades, McGovern did return home unscratched, through whatever combination of skill, luck, and the grace of God. He was a brave and skillful flier who earned the Distinguished Flying Cross, among other decorations. While on active duty, he unfailingly persevered in the performance of his duties, with modesty and without complaint. He served his country well.

Don Perry, Nell Perry, Eleanor McGovern, and George McGovern in front of Cadet Club in Coffeyville, Kansas, 1943 or 1944

When the war ended, like millions of his fellow veterans, McGovern picked up the threads of his life and moved on. He returned to South Dakota and to college, intending to become a historian. Soon enough, however, he embarked on a long and honorable career in American politics. As a soldier during World War II, McGovern had submitted to the dictates of the state, as most Americans did in those days. Representing South Dakota first in the House of Representatives and then in the Senate, he did not submit, instead courageously challenging the prevailing orthodoxies of the Cold War.

We remember McGovern today chiefly as an unsuccessful presidential candidate, an opponent of the Vietnam War overwhelmingly defeated by Richard Nixon in 1972. Although perhaps understandable, this inclination is deeply inappropriate. To evaluate a life based on the basis of unmet aspirations is necessarily to overlook what a person actually accomplished. In McGovern's case, those accomplishments, stretching across many decades of service to his country, were formidable.

That service began in wartime. In this brief document, replete with artwork and aphorisms that evoke the era from which it comes to us, we get a sense of the man he was to become. We also come to understand why McGovern, having experienced combat at first hand, was not in later life among those given to glorifying war or to sending their fellow citizens to fight when not absolutely necessary.

McGovern climbing into a training aircraft, 1943

EDITOR'S NOTE

On the following pages is George McGovern's World War II diary exactly as he wrote it, hastily jotted down between bombing missions whenever he had the impulse and the time to put his thoughts on paper. We chose to reprint it here just as he wrote it in order to convey the immediacy of his wartime experiences. For ease of reading, we have also included a print transcription that is a duplicate of the handwritten diary, with its inconsistencies as well as its spelling and grammatical errors. We are confident that readers will not be bothered by these inconsistencies, perhaps not even notice them, and will be as enthralled as we are by the experiences of this true American hero—a man who, in the pages of *Harper's Magazine*, responded to the self-styled patriots of his day who proclaimed "America, love it or leave it" with "America, let us improve it so that we may love it the more."

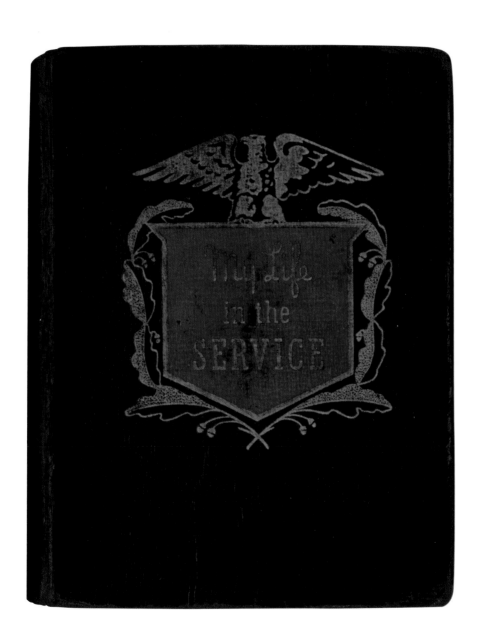

My Life in the SERVICE

13

ARMY INSIGNIA

George S. McGovern

General	Lieut. Gen.	Maj. Gen.	Brig. Gen.

Aviation Observer's Badge

Military Intelligence

Quartermaster

Pilot's Badge

Military Police

Inspector Gen.

Chaplain (Christ.)

Senior Pilot's Badge

Infantry

General Staff

Medical Corps

Chaplain (Jewish)

Command Pilot's Badge

Cavalry

Coast Artillery

Signal Corps

Sanitary Reserves

Colonel

Field Artillery

Chemical Warfare

Nurses Corps

Lieut. Col. (silver)

Major (gold)

Master Sergeant

Air Corps and Flying Cadet

Aide to Brig. Gen.

Medical Admin.

Captain

1st Lieut. (silver)

2nd Lieut. (gold)

Engineers

Ordnance

Veterinary

Dental Corps

Warrant Officer

Private 1st Class

Corporal

Regular Sergeant

Staff Sergeant

Technical Sergeant

First Sergeant

14

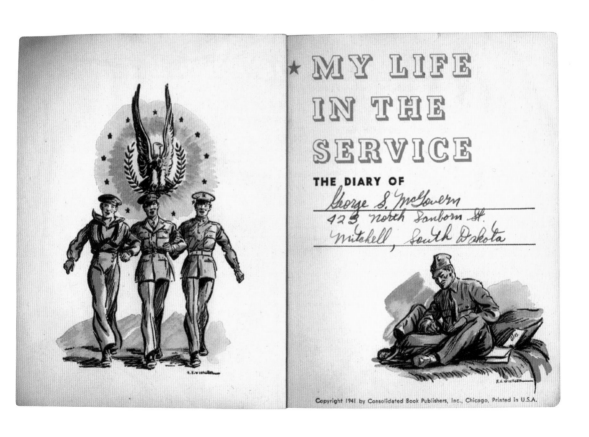

★ MY LIFE IN THE SERVICE

THE DIARY OF

George S. McGovern
423 north Sanborn St.
Mitchell, South Dakota

Your experiences in the armed forces of your country are your part of living history. By all means KEEP A DIARY! Times without number, historians and writers have found more information of real human interest in the diaries of enlisted men than in the studied accounts of generals and admirals. This book, conscientiously kept, may prove to be the living record of your destiny five hundred years from now!

By keeping a diary, you provide a record that can be referred to in after years for verification should any question arise. Although the Army, Navy, and Marines keep official records of all the men in the armed forces, there are many ways in which their records can be lost or destroyed in time of war. Your personal record may supply vital information that is available at no other source.

It is particularly essential to record any disability or hospital treatment received, whether on duty or on leave. This should be a detailed account—giving dates, names of Medical Officers and Examining Physicians—with complete facts concerning hospitalization.

Because the events recorded in these pages are likely to be the most significant of your life, and the ones most worthy of remembrance, DON'T TRUST THEM TO MEMORY.

Keep a written record. You will be glad you did so—countless times—when you have need to recall incidents, places, dates, and close companions. In many cases diaries have been turned to profit for their authors: newspapers and magazines have published them—with permission from the War or Navy Department—to give their readers a true, firsthand picture of service life.

Especially planned for convenience, this book has designated pages for every pertinent entry—names, addresses, dates, places, people, autographs, and photographs. By all means PHOTOGRAPHS! One picture is said to be worth a thousand words . . . get as many pictures as you can, of people and places, for an illustrated diary is the best of all!

And if for any reason it becomes inadvisable for you to keep your diary with you, if your duties are such that the book should not be in your possession, DON'T STOP MAKING ENTRIES! Send your diary home or to a friend for safekeeping. Then while you are away, send your entries home in letters—regularly. Keep your diary up to date by proxy.

Remember, the value of this record lies in the future; the time to create that value is now. Resolve to make an entry, however short, EVERY SINGLE DAY! Make this book a treasure trove of rich memories.

MOUNT
PHOTO
HERE

MY PHOTOGRAPH, taken_____
Where   When

IDENTIFICATION

Name _George S. McGovern_

Rank _____ Serial Number _17098393_

Unit _____

Stationed at _____

Religion _Wesleyan Meth. - Christian_

Date of Birth _7 - 19 - 1922_ Weight _165_

Color _White_   Color of Hair _Brown_

Height _5'11½"_   Color of Eyes _Blue_

Birthmarks or Other Distinguishing Features _____

_____

_____

NEAREST RELATIVE OR FRIEND

Name _Joseph C. McGovern (father)_

Address _423 North Sanborn St._

City _Mitchell_   State _So. Dak._

★ SERVICE RECORD ★
TRANSFERS AND CHANGES IN RANK

Left home Feb. 19, 1943 to Omaha, Neb.
Omaha, Neb. Feb 20. to Jefferson Bks. Mo.
Jeff. Bks, Mo. Mar. 22 '43 Carbondale, Ill. S.I.N.U.

★ PHYSICAL RECORD

ON ENTERING THE SERVICE

Date 2-20-1943 Weight_____

Chest—Normal_____ Expanded_____ Waist_____

Date_____
Weight_____
Chest—Nor._____ Exp._____
Waist_____

Date_____
Weight_____
Chest—Nor._____ Exp._____
Waist_____

Date_____
Weight_____
Chest—Nor._____ Exp._____
Waist_____

Date_____
Weight_____
Chest—Nor._____ Exp._____
Waist_____

Date_____
Weight_____
Chest—Nor._____ Exp._____
Waist_____

Date_____
Weight_____
Chest—Nor._____ Exp._____
Waist_____

Date_____
Weight_____
Chest—Nor._____ Exp._____
Waist_____

Date_____
Weight_____
Chest—Nor._____ Exp._____
Waist_____

Date_____
Weight_____
Chest—Nor._____ Exp._____
Waist_____

Date_____
Weight_____
Chest—Nor._____ Exp._____
Waist_____

Date_____
Weight_____
Chest—Nor._____ Exp._____
Waist_____

Date_____
Weight_____
Chest—Nor._____ Exp._____
Waist_____

CITATIONS, AWARDS AND DECORATIONS

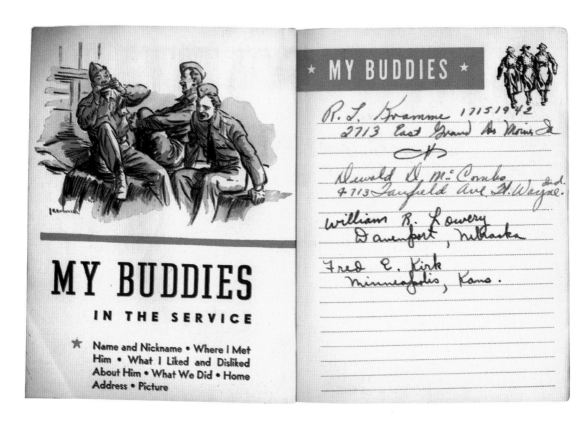

MY BUDDIES

IN THE SERVICE

★ Name and Nickname • Where I Met Him • What I Liked and Disliked About Him • What We Did • Home Address • Picture

★ MY BUDDIES ★

R. S. Kramme 171519 42
2713 East Grand Des Moines Ia

Dewald D. McCombe
4713 Fairfield Ave Ft. Wayne. Ind.

William R. Lowery
Davenport, Nebraska

Fred E. Kirk
Minneapolis, Kans.

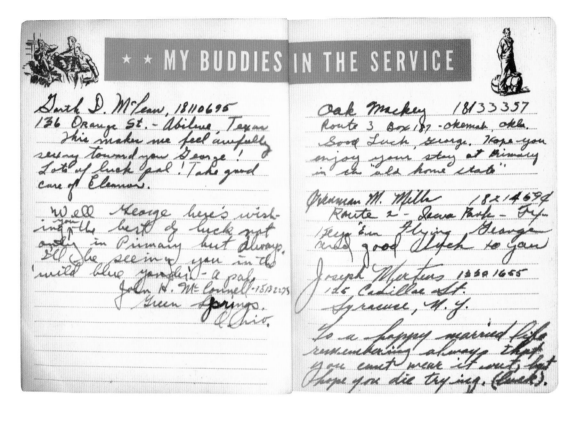

Garth D. McLean, 18110695
136 Orange St. - Abilene, Texas
   This makes me feel awfully
sorry toward you George!
Lots of luck, pal! Take good
care of Eleanor.

   Well George here's wish-
ing you the best of luck not
only in Primary but always.
I'll be seeing you in the
"wild blue yonder" - a pal.
            John H. McConnell - 15132273
                  Green Springs,
                        Ohio.

Oak Mackey   18133357
Route 3 Box 187 - Okemah, Okla.
Good Luck, George. Hope you
enjoy your stay at Primary
in the "old home state"

Freeman M. Mills   18214694
   Route 2 - Sand Park - Tep-
seu 'em Flying George
and good luck to you

Joseph Mertens 13591655
125 Cadillac St.
Syracuse, N.Y.

To a happy married life
remembering always that
you can't wear it out but
I hope you die trying. (luck).

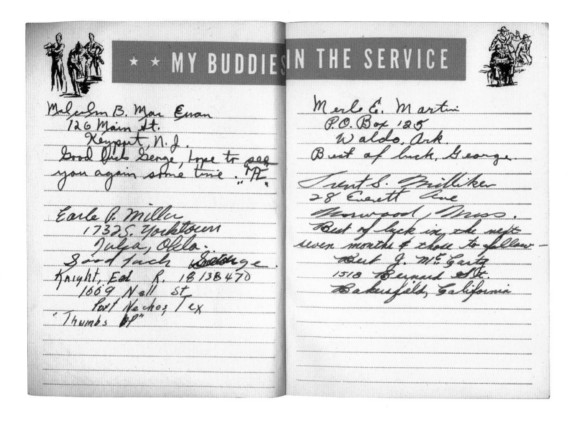

Malcolm B. Mac Ewan
126 Main St.
Kenport, N.J.
Good luck George, hope to see
you again some time. "R."

Earle P. Miller
1732 S. Yorktown
Tulsa, Okla.
Good luck George.
Knight, Ed. R. 18138470
1669 Nall St
Port Neches Tex
"Thumbs Up"

Merle E. Martin
P.O. Box 125
Waldo, Ark.
Best of luck, George.

Trent S. Milliken
28 Everett Ave
Norwood, Mass.
Best of luck in the next
seven months & those to follow —
Bert J. McGarty
1518 Bernard St.
Bakersfield, California

Earl S. McVay
35 Hiawatha Ave
Westerville, Ohio

A lot of luck to a
swell fellow - "Mac."

Robert J. Martin
4 East 113th Place
Chicago, Illinois

Good Luck fellow you
deserve it "Bob."

Stanley R. Metsker
Kingman, Indiana

Best of Luck + wishes for a
happy future – a pal.

Robert L. Martin
3862 Lamont
San Diego, California

Paul Victor Medalo
2 Highland Street
(Indian) Massachusetts

Robert G. Mason
1609 Doone Rd.
Columbus 8, Ohio

Robert M. Josephson
Minneota, Minn.

Justin L. Berger
1318 So. 4 Ave.
Phone 6192
Sioux Falls, S. D.

Wm A. Mc Cormick
R.F.D. #1
Oakdale Penna. (near Pittsburgh)

John D. Lyding, Jr.
5725 Kimbark Ave.
Chicago, 37, Ill.

John P. Houserman Jr.
7514 Graymore Road
Pittsburgh, Penna.

Merl A. Lehenbauer
Ames, Oklahoma
Richard W. Jones
5 Hickory Ave. Takoma Pk. Md. or 207 E.
2nd N. Logan, Utah

Ted McGrath
4471 San Francisco St.
St. Louis, Mo.
Remember the guy who always beat
you dressed for S.M.I.

Paul G. McCammon
205 South 9th Street
Rocky Ford, Colo.
"Scraptie"

24

David Labeck
2020 s.w.4th ave
Miami Florida

Vernon C. Long
208 Plum St.
Tipton, Iowa

Harry B. Long
2012 Spruce St.
Philadelphia, Pa.

John M. Logue
760 Gallion ave
Pittsburgh, Pa.

Carl M. Linder Jr
4309 W. Franklin St.
Richmond, Virginia

Leon S. Hoffman Jr.
2415 Shafor Blvd.
Dayton, Ohio

Carl H. Hough
521 Spring St.
Brownsville, Penna.

Lloyd J. Fairbanks
Emmett, Kansas

Frank M. Guest
636 Stewart ave
New Hyde Pk L.I. N.Y.

25

Mr and Mrs. William B. Evans
1708 Sanderson Ave.
Scranton, Pa.

a/c Fred R. Pittera & Mrs.
206 Main Street
Middletown, Connecticut

Mr. and Mrs. Chas. D. Ohle
Hadley, Penna.

Mr & Mrs. Albert A. Cape
770 Broad St.
Conneaut Ohio

Mr. & Mrs. Owen J. Lyons
212 So. Vermillion
Streator Ill.

S/c Mrs. Donald H. Perry
2269 Cooley Avenue
Palo Alto, California

1/c Burton C. Smith
411 South Dartmouth
Albuquerque, New Mexico

a/c Lawrence E. Olsen
10539 So. Bell Ave.
Chicago, Illinois

A/c John S. McClelland
208 S. Catherine St. - 6-2796
Mobile, Ala.

Mr & Mrs. R. M. Mabry
Dublin, Mississippi

26

4/c Cameron K. Lyon,
    Pierpont, Ohio

4/c John E. Mc Davis
        Inola, Okla.

Hugh L. McCracken
1225 Berkshire Ave
Pgh. Pa.

Mr. and Mrs. Hugh R. McFarland
    728 Willa St   Mt Washington
        Pittsburgh, Pa.
(Call HE 0903 anytime.)

    William D. Mc Donald
        Taylor Ave.
            Falls Creek Pa.

William E. Lukey
444 W. Grand
Decatur 20, Illinois

Lt. Lewis R. Bevers
10 32 1. E 11
Okla. City, Okla.

Mrs. Lewis R. Bevers
26 2 3 N. Dewey
Okla. City, Okla.

Lt. James D. Mallory
549 Van Buren St.
Gary, Indiana

Robert C Sanderson
Mount Vernon,
Iowa

27

★ ★ MY BUDDIES IN THE SERVICE

Lt. & Mrs. Russell T. Greer
Mt. Royal Blvd.
Glenshaw, Penna.
(outside of Pittsburgh)

Charles Y. Herdman
℅ J. Paul Herdman
211 So. Le Doux
Beverly Hills, Calif.

Marion Z Culver
1106 State St   ℅ J. W. Culver
New Orleans, La   same address

Vervin R. Gilson
320 N. 1st West
Payson Utah

OFFICERS
I HAVE MET

★ Name and Address • His Rank • Home Address • His Picture if Possible • What I and Others Liked and Disliked About Him

Crew 6635
Copilot - Ralph C. "Bill" Rounds
4c, No. Roosevelt St. Wichita, Kans.
c/o R. M. Rounds
Navigator Charles S. Adams "Sam"
% Mrs. Janet Rundle
2211 E. Kenwood Blvd.
Milwaukee 11, Wisconsin

Bombardier William S. Eames "Bill"
% Mrs & Mr. John W. Eames
Star Route
Roberts Idaho

CIVILIANS
I HAVE MET WHILE IN THE SERVICE

★ Name • Address • Picture • Phone Number • How and Why Our Acquaintance Started • General Comment and Things to Remember

Dr. Harvey D. D.
Methodist Minister
First Methodist church
Carbondale, Ill.

Mr. & Mrs. Cromeans
509 S. Normal
Carbondale, Ill.

Mrs. Thrailkill
Carbondale, Ill.
(Has a son named Merrill who is a captain in the air corps).

Miss Betty Eckert
S. I. N. U. - Carbondale, Ill.

July 9, 1943. Carbondale, Illinois.

Dear Leo: All the best wishes in the world go with you as you leave us tonight. It has been wonderful to know you and if I had a son, I'd want him just like you. Keep your faith firm, and remember our thoughts and prayers will always follow you. Come & see us some day and always count our home as your home.

Your Pal & Friend,

M.S. Hanky

216 W. Main
First Methodist
Church.

THE FOLLOWING PAGES CONTAIN THE DIARY OF MY LIFE IN THE SERVICE

This simple record of my daily experiences and thoughts has given me pleasure in the writing of it. If for any reason it leaves my possession, I would like to have it forwarded to:

Name _George McGovern_

Address _423 N. Sanborn_

City _Mitchell_ State _S. D._

Our train was scheduled to leave Mitchell at 8 P.M. on Feb. 19, 1943. We were delayed about an hour and a half but spent the time visiting with students and faculty members from the college who came down to see us off. Most of my close friends, my family and the twins were there!

On the sleeper to Omaha we met a couple of air cadets who were going to Omaha with Kreiman and I. We pulled into Omaha about 10 a.m. Sat. Feb. 20.

At the induction center in Omaha we met Sgt. Francis Robbins whom

we ate dinner with. He
gave us some of the inside
dope which every man in the
army seems to know. By
the way the first lesson I
learned in the army is that
it's best to ignore all rumors
and the so-called inside dope.

We spent the afternoon in
Omaha at Nebraska's largest
theater — it was really beautiful.
The feature attraction was a stage
show by Chico Marx and his
orchestra. We got a bang out of it.

At 4 P.M. we got onto a
troop train with 250 other
air cadets. — all bound for
Jefferson Barracks Mo. In
spite of the fact that it
took us until 6. A.M. the

34

next day to get to J. B. and we neither slept nor ate during this trip, I really enjoyed it. The fellows were all in a good mood. I was told and it was easily apparent that we had the cream of the crop in our outfit. We were all college men — mostly juniors and seniors. Walt and I met two fellows whom we got to know fairly well on the train — Russ Feikes from Vermillion and Chuck Burke from Pierre.

Upon our arrival at J. B. we were led to the general mess hall for a top-notch breakfast which really hit the spot. Everywhere we

Every man thinks meanly of himself for not having been a soldier.—*Samuel Johnson*

35

went in the camp we heard the cry " You won't like it here."

It seems that due to the wet, changing weather nearly everyone had a bad cold. Hundreds of the fellows were down with pneumonia — many had died. I've resolved to be careful. The old veterans claim it'll get you, anyway.

We were then assigned to our huts — ten men to each hut. Walt Kreiman & I who had stuck together since leaving Mitchell both managed to get in the same hut — in fact the same double bunk. He in the upper berth. I in the lower.

Righteousness exalteth a nation.
—Proverbs XIV: 34

After getting our blankets, we learned how to make up an army bunk. Every fold must be just so, or K.P. is the result. Also the hut must be kept in perfect order, or we are deprived of our passes into St. Louis. That was our second lesson — the army is precise and exacting. Everything is done according to army methods.

I also discovered that in the army everybody gripes about everything from the weather to the food. It's just the soldiers way of relaxing and getting rid of tension. As yet we have had nothing to gripe about. Our "Sarg" is O.K. He's more lenient than most of them.

We met Bob Muchy this evening, and some other fellows ~~this~~ from Mitchell. Red Fuller lives across the street from our hut, so we have plenty of company. It makes it easier to start out with fellows you know. All the boys are friendly, though, and its easy to get acquainted. We've got some A-1 fellows in our hut. One of them is married.

After writing a few letters we turned in and the first day in camp was over. In spite of the continuous cry "You won't like it here", we enjoyed the first day thoroughly. Here's hoping it won't get any worse, but it probably will. They tell us we are really in earnest about this war.

Mar. 2, 1943

After 10 days at J.B. we find that it is getting easier for us all the time as we learn some of the tricks and methods of the army. We have sore arms from our first 3 shots for vaccinations! Received a card from Bob Mucky who has been transferred to Coe College, Iowa. We hope soon to join him.

Those letters from home are really helping a lot — especially the love letters. Mail is more valuable than food in the army.

We had the day off because of a snow storm which made it impossible to drill. Our swell sergeant got us out of detail work by a few white lies

The less there is of fear, the less there is of danger.—*Livy*

to the top sergeant.

We had our first real inspection
of huts and lockers today and
passed with flying colors.

Mar. 5, 1943

Well, we are all nursing
some very sore arms tonight having
received our second vaccinations today.
We also passed our second real
inspection. Yesterday we were confined to our area because some
hut in our Flight C wasn't clean,
but we are out again tonight.
Six of the boys in our platoon 1504
were shipped out today. The rest of
us are anxiously hoping for the
day when we will get our shipping
orders. Dick Nash, hut mate, included in 6

We have completed all our
drill maneuvers and now it is

simply a matter of practice until we become proficient.
Got my daily letter from Eleanor.
How I wait for her mail and
the other mail from home. Wrote
a lot of letters myself the last
few days.

Today we got something that
all of us have been hoping for—
shipping orders. our whole flight
except for the sick boys is to
leave tomorrow. Rumors are
flying thick and fast as to where
we are going. Some say west Virginia,
others Illinois, still others Wisconsin.
At any rate we are all glad to be
going. Our month of training at
Jefferson Barracks has
been very valuable, but

Confidence begets confidence.—*Proverb*

41

also very hard and sometimes
discouraging. Most of us had
bad colds or other ills while we
were here. Due to the location
of the camp on the mississippi
River just at the south edge of
St. Louis it is damp here and
disease spreads easily.

To list some of the things we
have done at J. B. I could mention
the following things: First of all
we learned a lot about drilling.
Sergeant Trumbo is a very good
drill man and he succeeded in
making us one of the best drill
platoons on the post.

Secondly we learned to fire
an army Springfield rifle! our
first day on the rifle range was
perhaps one of our most enjoyable

Almost everything that is great has been done by youth.
—Disraeli

Days at J. B. We also were given a chance to fire a clip in the army's Thompson Sub-Machine Gun. I myself, was too excited to be very accurate with the piece, but better luck next time.

Gas mask drill — another event at J. B. After being carefully instructed in the use of the gas mask we were marched over to the gas chamber and subjected to 15 minutes of tear gas. Then we took off our masks for 30 seconds to get a "taste" of tear gas. Needless to say we were all crying for the next half hour. At least we had learned to appreciate the army's gas mask — the finest in the world.

When we assumed the soldier, we did not lay aside the citizen.—*George Washington*

One of our most interesting drills at J.B. was bayonet practice. Using wooden guns we were taught and practiced thrusts, jabs, vertical and horizontal butt kicks and smashes, and other bayonet tactics. This is one type of fighting I think would be worse than any other. After bayonet practice two of the boys in our platoon showed us a little jiu jitsu. I managed to pick up a few holds that I think may be useful some day.

We also mastered the manual of arms which is the various positions and movements of the rifle.

After going over to medical four

When duty whispers low, *Thou must,*
The youth replies, *I can.—Emerson*

44

cines for typhoid, small pox
and tetanus shots our arms
were pretty well poked full
of holes. We now feel fairly
well protected against almost
every disease imaginable.

After two weeks of processing
we were given passes into St.
Louis any day of the week. I
managed to get in several times
before we left. Walt Kreiman
and I heard the St. Louis
Symphony with Artur Rubenstein
at the piano. He was very good.
The high light of the entertainment
in St. Louis, however, was a
concert by Marian Anderson. We
service men and women were all
seated behind Miss Anderson on
the stage — a great honor we
thought.

She turned around and sang
several numbers to us and
the audience applauded loudly.
The concert was marvelous.
Probably the best music I have
ever heard. I succeeded in
getting Miss Anderson's autograph which I sent to Oline.

I shall never forget the
fine facilities of the U. S. O. Center
in St. Louis. They have everything for the soldiers enjoyment.
We could take showers, press
our clothes, shave, play ping
pong, play the piano, read,
write letters, make phone calls,
get invitations to private homes,
play games or almost any-
thing imaginable. If we so
wished there were hostesses for

46

everyone who wanted company.

St. Louis is the eighth largest city in the U.S. and I imagine one of the oldest. It has several beautiful parks. I visited Forest Park and Shaws Gardens - two of the most beautiful places in the world.

This then, has been some of things that took up our time at Jefferson Barracks. It has been a very busy eventful month. Those were awfully long days from 5 a.m. to 9 P.M. every day of the week. It has been good for us though, especially the housemaid duties. Incidentally I almost forgot to mention K.P. I spent this much dreaded day taking trays full of dishes

Let it be your pride to show all men everywhere not only what good soldiers you are, but also what good men you are.—*Woodrow Wilson*

from a steam dish washer.
It was really a tough day. One
that I'll always remember.
I must not forget to mention
guard duty. This wasn't so bad.
I had the watch from 2 to 4 a.m.
only the novelty of the job for
excitement on my part.

And now a little description
of our huts. At first there were
only ten of us to a hut but
later only eight. The huts were
rude wooden structures about
eighteen by eighteen feet. There
was no furniture in the room
except our bunks and our lockers.
These huts were hard to keep
clean: so we had to mop them
or G.I. them every morning
It was really a sight to see

A mysterious bond of brotherhood makes all men one.
—*Carlyle*

us all pushing mops at 5 a.m. in the morning. We also had to keep a fire in our stoves all the time as the huts were full of cracks and the air was chilling and damp.

My first hut mates were the following boys: Laird Loomis, U. of Missouri; Leslie Livingston, U. of Neb.; Darrell Huth, U. of Neb.; Dick Nash, U. of Neb.; Homer Livermore, Uni. of Neb.; Bill Lowery, Uni. of Neb.; Bill Lukely, Creighton Uni.; Walter Kriman, D.W.U. I lived with these boys for two weeks. The second two weeks were spent with these boys (colleges follow names): Chuck Little, Hastings College; Don Linnaman, Peru College; (cont.)

Wallace "Rocky" Lake, Hastings Col.;
Percy Kirkely, Augustana; Don
Lee, Iowa State College; Dave
Hescher, Midland college; and
one of the old hut mates Homer
Livermore, Univ. of Neb. A few
days before we left J. B. Homer
was taken sick and had to go
to the hospital. He was still
there when we were leaving.
My first hut mates were very
congenial and we got along
fine, but the next fellows
were hard to get along with.
All in all we managed pretty
well, however.

    This then completes the
story of a month at Jefferson
Barracks. It has been good
training, but we are all

heaving a sigh of relief that
it is in the past.

March 26, 1943
well, one of the rumors
was right. We are in Carbondale,
Illinois. We arrived here on
Tuesday. This college
is Southern Illinois State
Normal University. It is a
beautiful old college and campus.
Seems heavenly compared to
old J. B. First, however, a
word about our trip down
here. We first clambered
into a fleet of army trucks
like a bunch of excited kids
and were whisked down to
the shipping depot. There we
were given "short arm" inspection

while everyone held his breath
for fear he had a temperature.
A temperature meant being
scratched from the shipping
list — too bad for a few boys.
        After passing inspection we
were loaded onto a very crowded
troop train and taken into St.
Louis. From there we transferred
to a larger and far better train
and came directly to Carbondale, arriving about 5 P. M.
        So far life here has been
rather monotonous for me as
I have been confined to quarters
because of a pleuresy in the
region around my left eye.
It is better today so I hope
                to be on the go
                again tomorrow.

Valor is the soldier's adornment.—*Livy*

I can see that the military discipline is going to be more than strict here. It is almost unbelievable to see how ~~much~~ rigid they are in enforcing the thousand and one military rules here. We must even walk at attention in the halls and on the campus. We can eat only with our right hand, etc.

My room-mate is busy polishing our brass door knobs for inspection. Maybe this idea of reporting for sick call isn't so bad after all. It's pretty convenient to have orders to stay in bed while your buddy does your work for you. I'd still like to be up, however,

Worth, courage, honor, these indeed
Your sustenance and birthright are.—*E. C. Stedman*

Last night of a box of home made fudge came in from Eleanor and Mildred. Gee is it ever good. I'd like to kiss them both for it, but then that will have to wait. By the way, it would really be nice to be home for awhile. I'm slightly homesick today. Wish I could see Eleanor and my mother for awhile. Sent them a telegram last night. My roommate from J.B. and Nebraska University, Bill Lowery wrote Eleanor a letter for me last night as my eye was bothering me.

Where liberty dwells there is my country.
—Benjamin Franklin

June 12, 1943

Today everyone in flight I is rejoicing. After three months of hitting the books we begin to fly. Today we moved back to old Anthony Hall from University courts. Bill and I still managed to be room-mates. Walt Kreiman and his group having completed their required 10 hours of flying left for San Antonio today. Bill & I have his old room.

June 26, 1943

Finished ten hours of flying that we are to get in Carbondale. I had forgotten nearly all that I knew about flying in the time since I took CPT. at

It is better to lose a battery than a battle.
—*General Zachary Taylor*

the end of the ten hours though
I felt capable of taking "her"
up and landing alone. no
solo flight here though. will
have to wait until later for
that. looks as though our
remaining two weeks in
Carbondale at S.I.N.U. will
be spent pretty much at ease.
only three classes a day. we
sleep all morning.

Jumping back a month
to May 28, 1943 I must record
my first army furlough. after
getting a letter from mother
saying that dad was quite low
I was given a ten day furlough.
nothing ever made me happier
than a chance to go home for

awhile. It seemed to me that the train for Mitchell never would get there although in reality we made very good time. I rode the Hiawatha from Chicago into Sioux Falls and hitch-hiked from there to Mitchell in the middle of the night—Foolish but the only thing I could do to get home as soon as I wanted to. The week at home was a dream but I came back with soaring spirits and a new drive to work. Wish the air corps could give more furloughs. I was especially glad to get home because the blood transfusion that I gave to dad seemed to help him.

Fight the good fight of faith.
—I Tim. VI: 12

July 10, 1943

At 2 A.M. this morning we left Carbondale for San Anth. I spent my last evening in Carbondale visiting CromCorn and Dr. Harvey. They were very good to me during my stay at S. I. N. U. and did a lot to make me enjoy life at Carbondale. It was hard to say goodbye to these swell people and the friendly spirit of Carbondale. The town had very few entertainment facilities but the hospitality of the people more than made up for that. I was invited out to dinner six or seven different Sundays to various church homes The meals were wonderful and the friendliness of the people is

the greater than any place I've
ever been. Some day I'd like
to go back to this little town
in southern Illinois and visit
the people who treated us so
swell and the old college
where we spent what will
probably be our three and a half
happiest months in the army.
The faculty was not too
strong but our military and
physical training program was
of the best.

July 11, 1943
Deep in the heart of Texas.
We arrived here about 4:30 this
afternoon after an enjoyable trip.
It hard to believe but the
army actually arranged sleepers
for us on this trip. We

Do your duty in all things. You cannot do more. You
should never wish to do less.—*Robert E. Lee*

Came by way of Memphis
and New Orleans which
made it possible for me to
go through four states I had
never been in before. we
were in New Orleans and
Memphis each for a couple
of hours, but had very little
chance to see the towns.
Most of the boys had their first
experience of being propositioned
by negro chippies in New
Orleans.

July 14, 1943
Today we started our
classifications to determine
whether we will be a pilot, a
navigator, or a bombardier. we
took the seven hour
mental test today

We have room for but one loyalty, loyalty
to the United States.

—Theodore Roosevelt

under enough pressure to put some fellows on their backs.

The next day we get our psychomotor test which tests our coordination and reaction time. We are run through a series of all different kinds of weird looking machines which help to determine whether or not we have the stuff to become air crew members.

Following this comes the air corps famous No. 64 physical in which they go over us from head to toe. Only a perfect physical specimen can get through this maze of doctors and apparatus. Needless to say, I'm praying that I'll get through! The sisuu

The cause of freedom is the cause of God.—*W. L. Bowles*

trouble which I developed at J.B. may cause me some trouble.

July 15, 1943

There are four of us here in our barracks from Carbondale—Bill Lowery, Wilmer Randon, Fred Kirk and myself. We are in a barracks right next to the orderly room but that doesn't prevent us from using this classification period as an ideal time to gold brick for about 3 weeks

Aug 1, 1943

Finally got to pre flight after being classified as a pilot. Seems like a quiet place but the discipline is terrific.

oct 1, 1943

arrived is Muskogee for primary.
we are now real pilots.

oct. 16, 1943

My first solo flight as an
army pilot — a day I'll never
forget. This is the thing I've
been dreaming about for a long
time. I can now don the
wings of a solo pilot.

oct 27, 1943

Just passed my 20 hour
progress check ride given to
me by flight commander
Dixon. Its a relief to know
I was able to get by the check
boss. Check rides are tough as
a good percentage of our boys
can testify who washed out on
them.

Dec. 6, 1943

Arrived at Coffeyville, Kansas for basic. This place is a far cry from the modern barracks and country club atmosphere of Brinkary. It seems to be taken for granted that basic will be rough.

Feb. 8, 1944

Basic is over. Wasn't as tough as we prophesied, but we've learned a lot about flying in the fast nine weeks. Eleanor and I will Perry left last night to drive to Pampa, Texas where we are going for advanced.

Feb. 9, 1944
We left Coffyville on Pullmans last night arriving in Pampa this morning. From all reports it is likely to be pretty tough going for awhile here. Realizing that will be through in nine weeks, however, will keep morale high no matter how tough it gets.

April 15, 1944
Wings & commission at last. Now for an eleven day delay enroute before reporting to Liberal Kansas for B-24 transition beginning April 27.

Dare, will, keep silence.
—William Bolitho

65

June 9, 1944 - Finished transition and flew to Lincoln, Nebraska today. Will be assigned a crew here.

June 25, - '44 Drove to Mt. Home, Idaho with Don & Nell Perry and Joe Herdman. Ready now for the real combat training.

Sept. 17 - 1944 - Finished all three phases of combat training with my crew at Mt. Home. We graduated today and will leave tomorrow for Topeka, Kans. for overseas assignment and a possible flyaway.

And you can win, though you face the worst,
If you feel that you're going to do it.—*Edgar A. Guest*

Oct 1, 1944 — We spent about a week at Topeka including a four day pass which Eleanor spent with me. We stayed at the Kansan Hotel as did the Round's. Met Commander Standish Hall and his wife who are Wichita friends of the Round's. Mr. Rounds put on a wonderful crew banquet for us at the Kansan.

There were 41 crews in our group of which 30 were sent immediately to a P.O.E. for embarkation. The remaining 11 of us are now on our way to Langley Field, Va. to get our overseas assignment there. Why the move, we don't know.

Oct. 5, 1944 - We didn't get a flyaway at Langley, but merely waited about five days there. Russ Greer, Sparks, Blanton, Sanderson & some of the others in our group did get flyaways but the last three on the list who were Joe Herdman, Don Perry, & I myself are going over by boat. We moved to Camp Patrick Henry today — a camp just about 20 miles from Langley Field.

Oct. 13, 1944 - We boarded our ship tonight at Hampton Roads P.O.E. near Newport News.

And though hard be the task,
Keep a stiff upper lip.—*Phoebe Cary*

Oct. 14, 1944 – We slipped out of port early this morning, but after spending the day joining with other ships to form a convoy we find ourselves just a few miles off shore from where we left and we don't put out to sea for good until about 8. P. M. this evening. The convoy seems to be moving southward to pick up still more ships.

Oct. 25 1944 – This forenoon we passed through the strait of Gibralter. It was a bright clear day and we had a good view of Gibralter on our left and Africa on our right. We are now following

A republic may be called the climate of civilization.
—*Victor Hugo*

a route along the coast of
Africa. our destination was
announced several days ago
as Naples, Italy but nevertheless
we are holding close to the
north african coast of the
mediterranean.
Oct 26, 1944 - Still flowing
along the north african coastline.
It is a continuous line of
rugged mountainous country
along the coast and has
been in view ever since
we entered the mediterranean
yesterday morning. we still
have our convoy of about
25 ships — mostly cargo ships
tankers, troop ships and two
or three escorting destroyers.
we picked up some of these

Sloth, like rust, consumes faster than labor wears.
—Benjamin Franklin

ships several days out at sea. All of the ships including ours are armed even though it is light armament. We are armed with a couple of 75 millimeter guns and a group of 20 millimeters scattered from stern to stern. Occasionally a protective blimp or a naval patrol plane checks up to see that we are O.K. or perhaps just to add a little interest to their monotonous patrols.

Oct. 28, 1944

Landed in Naples harbor today. Saw Isle of Capri & Mt. Vensuvius coming in. Will spend tonight on board ship. Move to classification and shipping center tomorrow morning.

oct. 29   '44

Moved to classification base
near Caserta, Italy & Naples.
Had our first experience in
sleeping under a tent during
Italy's well known rainy season

oct. 30 - '44

Visited Caserta & Naples.
People seem rather aimless and
defeated looking. American cigarette
will buy almost anything.

oct. 31   '44

Arrived at Bari, Italy today.
Seems like a nice place.

nov. 1,   '44

We were taken by trucks today
to our permanent squadrons. It
rained all day and to make
matters worse there was no
tent for us. We found an
old tent which we put up

The sound body is a product of the sound mind.
—G. B. Shaw

ourselves. The nights here are plenty cold and damp so I imagine will work on a stove tomorrow.

Nov. 5, 1944

This squadron is reorganizing and as usual we come into it at the wrong time. The Italians have been hired to build a rock and cement floor for our tents. We do the rest. Namely, build stoves chairs, tables, washstands and anything else to make life enjoyable here. We have succeeded in bartering with the Italians for such things as lamps, floor matts, dishes, etc.

Let brotherly love continue.
—New Testament

nov. 1944

Flew a formation practice mission today with a copilot named Kelleher. Weather forced us to land at another base where I learned that the entire flight I flew with at Mt. Home are here in the 15th. I saw Sandy and several of my other buddies.

nov.

We have a system here whereby each pilot must fly five combat missions with an experienced crew before he can go out with his own crew. I had my first one today with Lt. Moreman's crew. Weather kept us from getting clear into the target, but because of the difficulty we encountered with the weather those of us who stuck with the formation were given credit for the mission. Our wing lost ten ships because of the severe icing and rough weather encountered. It was worse than flak. Target was Linz, Germany

Nov. 16, 1944

Started out today for Munich, my second mission, but we had to turn back because of a defective turbo. Lt. Bone's crew was the one I flew with today.

Nov. 17 1944

Got credit for No. 2 today. We were scheduled to hit the no. 1 target of importance in Europe which is the huge oil refinery at Blechhammer Germany. This is a heavily defended target and

the flak is usually plenty
rough. We were held up again
by the weather though I had
to bomb our secondary target
which was the railroad yards
at Gyor, ~~Hungary~~. I flew
with Lt. Asa's crew today.
Flak wasn't too bad.

                    Nov. 18, 1944
    No 3. Today. We really did
a job today. Plastered the large
German airfield at Vicenza,
Italy. Nothing was left of the
runways or the installations when
we left. We also caught a lot
of planes parked on the airfield.
I flew with Lt. Armellino who
was a buddy of mine at C. T. D. in
        Carbondale, Ill.

Democracy is better than tyranny.
                    —Periander

Nov. 19, 1944

No. 4 - I feel guilty taking credit for this mission today. We couldn't find the target so came back with all our bombs. There was a heavy undercast over the target and the radar ship was unable to pick up the target beneath it. The target was a large heavily defended locomotive works at Verona, Italy. I flew with Asa again today.

Nov. 20, 1944

Completed No. 5. today. Again with Asa's crew. That means I can take up my own crew the next time and for the remaining thirty missions. Ralph has picked up four missions all with Lt. Moreman and Sam has one with Lt. Surbeck. The

He who is not prepared today, will be less so tomorrow.
—Ovid

rest of the crew have no missions.
They are ready to go now
however, as they were checked
out on a practice gunnery
mission today.

Again today the weather stopped
us from reaching Blechhammer.
We hit a rubber factory at Zlin
Czechoslovakia — a town about 80 miles
short of our intended target. One
of Asa's gunners finished his
missions off today and I got the
usual grease job by the ground
crew.

Nov. 21, 1944
Flew a practice mission with my
own crew today. Have been playing
touch football in the afternoons
lately. It's our main recreation
here!

Dec. 6, 1944

Same old story. We didn't hit our target — again because of the weather. We were supposed to hit Graz, Austria — the railroad yards. This would have taken a lot of pressure off the Yugoslavs and the Russians ~~eventually~~ because it is a funnel for supplies to the Germans in Yugo. We got credit for the mission — my sixth — because we were over enemy territory so long and encountered such rough weather. Our flight leader got separated from the main formation and took us down through some bad clouds over the Adriatic. Trying to stay in formation on instruments without being

79

able to see who you're following is no fun. It scared me worse than any flak I've seen yet. Incidentally I haven't encountered much flak yet and no enemy fighters. Our bombardier today was McGahran.

Dec. 9, 1944

Knocked off no. 7 today. We've been trying desperately to get through bad weather these past few days but again today we failed to make it. The formation turned back at the head of the Adriatic when we ran up against a wall of clouds 30,000 feet and higher over Germany. Our crew had a little excitement today. We were flying 166, an old baby that has seen its best days long ago. Just before the formation turned back we lost an engine — no. 3 — because of a cracked cylinder. I feathered the engine when the oil pressure fell off. We couldn't hold altitude nor stay with the formation. To make matters worse the weather had built up behind us so that I found myself in the soup & losing altitude on three engines with no. 1 also throwing oil badly. Our heaters were inoperative & we had been bitterly cold but needless to say I soon warmed up in all the fun. At first I decided to head for an emergency landing strip in

northern Italy but after
descending on instruments
through the soup to 12,000
feet no. 1 engine started
running smoothly, & also
we had lightened our load
by throwing out our ammunition
& dumping our bombs. I
was able to hold altitude O.K.
so decided to continue on the
three good engines with the
hope that no. 1 would hold
out O.K. If it hadn't I
knew we might very well
have to leave the crate. so
my navigator gave me a heading
that kept us close to the
coast at all times. we didn't
relish the idea of an ice
bath in the Adriatic. at any
rate everything turned out O.K.

Heroism feels and never reasons and therefore is always
right.—*Emerson*

I believe we learned more on this mission than anyone we have had yet.

Culver was our bombardier. This was his last mission. Our target was to have been the synthetic oil refinery at Moosbierbaum.

Dec. 13, 1944

Received the news of dad's death today. He died Dec. 7th according to the cable which took almost ten days to reach me. The news hit me pretty hard and came as a shock to me even though I knew dad was not well. I do know that he lived a beautiful life and died gloriously which is a great

Patriotism is a lively sense of collective responsibility.
—*Richard Aldington*

comfort now. He was the best man I ever knew and a wonderful dad. We'll miss him in a hundred ways, but he is happier now than ever before so we should not mourn his death too much.

Dec. 15, 1944

The mission which we had listed as no. 9 was taken away from us today because wing headquarters decided that we did not get close enough to the target to get credit for the mission.

We officially got no. 7 today though. Our target was the R. R. yards at Linz, Austria. Col. Keufer led the wing. Our plane flew on his left wing in no 3. spot.

Americanism consists in utterly believing in the principles of America.

—*Woodrow Wilson*

we had 917 today. Not a bad ship, but very stiff to handle so Ralph & I felt we had done a days work by the time we landed. Our bombardier was Duncan. I believe we did a good job over the target although the target was overcast. The mickey ship was able to get a fairly good scope of the target.

Dec. 16, 1944

Our target today — no. 8 — was one of the roughest targets in Europe — the synthetic oil refinery at Brux. It has over 250 flak guns concentrated in the oil refinery area which is the thickest flak in Europe. The air force is concentrating now on knocking out these synthetic

They never sought in vain that sought the Lord aright!
—R. Burns

oil plants because it is the very life blood of Germany's war machine. The terrific oil shortage in Germany has kept their planes grounded & their mechanized army at a much slower pace than would have been the case if they had plenty of oil. I flew no. 3 spot again today on Col. Thayer's wing. My copilot today was a new man who is being checked out - Lt. Brown. The bombardier was McGahran. We flew 279 today.

Dec. 17, 1944.
Another oil refinery today - the one at Oswiecim and Oderta in the Black-hammer flak area. This makes nine missions for me. We really got this one the hard way.

On our takeoff today we had a tire blow out - the right main gear tire, but it went out after we cleared the field or rather just as we left the field. We went on to the target knowing that we had a rough landing and perhaps a crack up waiting for us on our return. While going to the target we lost our manifold pressure on No. 2 engine but pulled enough power on the other three to go into the target and get back. The air force lost two ships to fighters and several to flak but we came through without a scratch. When we got back to the base I had everybody but the copilot, the

engineer, and myself go back
to the waist and brace them
selves for the landing. We
made sure that all loose
objects were tied down securely.
as soon as we touched the
runway I chopped the throttles
on the side of the good wheel
and advanced the throttles on
the side of the blown tire at
the same time holding down
the left brake. We made
the landing O.K. without
damaging the plane in the
least. needless to say old
terra firma felt plenty good.
My copilot today was Lt. Brown
and the bombardier was Lt.
McGahran. These two boys and I
Sam recommended me for the

Nothing is impossible to a valiant heart.
—Motto of Henry IV

D.F.C. because of the landing
but I don't feel as though I
deserve a medal as yet.

Dec. 18, '44

Oswiecim oil refinery today
for no. 10. My copilot today —
another new pilot was Arendt.
The bombardier McGahran. we
flew 26 (974) today. The mission
went off quite smoothly. no
one was lost to flak or fighters
I flew no. 3 again today. looks
as though that spot is reserved
for me. we hit Sopron, Austria instead
of ~~Oswiecim~~ due to bad weather.

Dec. 20 1944

I worked up a good sweat
again today. We had another rough
one — again in 279, the same
ship that I landed
on one wheel two days ago.

Ideals are the world's masters.
— J. G. Holland

Our target today was Brux, but
I lost an engine short of
the target. We had no sooner
started for home than I lost
No. 3 engine and I could not
feather it. The first engine
No. 2 came back in partially
after we came down from
altitude but in the meantime
No. 3 had caught fire. It continued to windmill until it
froze up. I could hold altitude
but couldn't depend on No. 2 which
was running rough. In addition
to that we were low on fuel
and the weather was bad. We
had a 1500 foot ceiling and
it was so hazy that the
navigator could hardly help
me at all. Sam was not

With firmness in the right, as God gives us to see the
right.—*Abraham Lincoln*

with me and the navigator
Lt. Vince apparently was unable
to do much of anything. Ralph
contacted "Big Fence" and they
gave us a heading to the
Isle of Viz — a little island
near the eastern side of the
Adriatic. We finally found
the island and located the
landing strip. It is a British
fighter strip and too short
for a heavy bomber to land
on, but we made it O.K. by
the grace of God. A C-47
which was taking off saw us
coming in; so they waited for
us to land and then brought
us back to our base.
    We lost several planes
and crews today in crash
landings due to the shortage

Obedience alone gives the right to command.—*Emerson*

91

of fuel and bad weather. one
of them is still unaccounted
for. This makes no. 11 for me.

Dec. 25, 1944

after briefing for four straight
days and not being able to get off
because of bad weather we finally
made it today. the air force
wanted to do everything possible to
give the Jerries a good plastering
on Christmas; so we took off in
spite of rain, muddy runways
and a ceiling of about 200 feet.
we flew out over the adriatic
in a column of ships stacked down
intrail of the lead ship. the ceiling
gradually raised as we headed north
to our rendezvous point at Via
              major welch was leading
          the group and to our

Presence of mind and courage in distress,
Are more than armies to procure success.
                              —Dryden

disappointment he turned around at the head of the adriatic — I came home because two of our boxes failed to make the rendezvous! I couldn't see his point — I we hated like the dickens to miss getting credit for the mission after working so hard to get through the weather. Our target was to have been Brux.

Dec. 26, 1944

Knocked off no. 12 today, the 15th Air Force is pledged to knock out Germany's synthetic oil production now that the loss of Ploesti has deprived her of her natural oil. We have already hit oil refineries at Brux, odertal, north — South Blechhammer, — I make our second smash

at Oswiecim today. The
flak was very heavy and
intense. Several planes were
shot up fairly bad but made
it back O.K. So make things worse
the lead navigator was off the
ball and took us over the
Bratislava flak area. We were
at 17,000 feet then and they
really scared the daylights out
of us. We picked up a nice
flak hole in the windshield
right in front of me. It
threw plexi glass all over
us but the piece of flak
didn't have our number on
it and went through the flight
deck into the bomb bay without
scratching any of us. It was
too close for comfort though.

Several flames really licked up some nice holes! A couple of the guys landed at Vis because of gasoline shortage or feathered engines. We really did a good job in knocking out the refinery. It was our first visual run in sometime!

Dec. 29 1944

Sam got back today after attending the "mickey" school at Bari for ten days. I will doubtless lose him now as he will be flying as a mickey operator in a radar ship from now on. With Ralph in the hospital with bronchitis for a couple of weeks I am pretty much alone as far as the officers on my crew are concerned.

The cement of this Union is the heart blood of every American.—*Thomas Jefferson*

Im afraid too that I may even lose, Mike, my engineer. He is 34 yrs. old and seems to be taking combat pretty hard. His nerves are bad and he is on edge most of the time. The flight surgeon told me today that he felt he would never make it through his tour unless he changed. The original boys are dropping out one by one. Eames was first to go when they took our bombardiers at Topeka. Siegel was next when I had him replaced the day we hit this squadron. Sam will be leaving us now to fly as a mickey man. If Ralph is checked out as a first pilot and mike goes out on us there won't be much left of my original crew.

We have met the enemy and they are ours.

—Oliver H. Perry

Jan. 31, 1945

After sitting around for over a month due to bad weather and an oversupply of crews to this squadron we finally got another mission. This one was to the oil refinery at Moosbierbaum. My copilot was Lt. Wynne and my navigator-bombardier Lt. Hassen. This was an ideal mission. No engine trouble, no surplus troms, and inaccurate flak. We flew Col. Keeler's wing in No. 3 spot for about the fourth time. It was a mickey run but I believe we laid our 'eggs right on the target. The mission was about the best all round mission I have been on. This was no. 13 for me.

No. 14 today. This was Hasser's last one. Lt. Reynolds was my copilot.

We flew No. 4 spot today. Our box leader lost the formation temporarily & we had to pull excessive power for about an hour to catch them. It seemed that an unusual amount of engine trouble hit our box today. When we got back to the base there were only 3 of the original 7 ships left in our box. The other four all either turned back or else had to lag the formation after bombs away.

We hit the marshalling yards and oil storage facilities at

He who commands the sea has command of everything.
—Themistocles

Regensburg Germany. Col.
Snowden led the group.

7 February 13, 1945
Vienna Matzliendor marshalling
yards was our target today. This
was our best mission I believe.
It was executed perfectly as
far as I am able to judge.
We had a visual run on
the target and the flak was
heavy and intense but no one
was hit bad. We picked up
three holes in our nose turret
and nose navigator's section but
luckily the flak fragments missed
connecting with anyone. John
Oxler flew as navigator for
me. Balth flew as copilot for
the first time in quite awhile.

Advantage is a better soldier than rashness.—H. G. Bohn

I cut the 15th notch today leaving 20 big ones yet to go. We plastered the target squarely this time.

February 18, 1945
Vienna Florisdorf oil Refinery was our objective today but weather kept us from reaching it. We were on instruments part of the time as it was. Turned back about the time we passed over the Alps. The Air Force was in a generous mood though and gave us credit for the mission making 16 for me. Lt. Barnes was our navigator. As usual we flew no. 3 slot.

When faith is lost, when honor dies,
The man is dead!—*Whittier*

Feb. 21, 1945

Vienna Central Marshalling Yds. made No. 17 for me today. This one took us right down main street on flak alley. No one was hit too badly though and we all got back to base. Lt. Cooper has been assigned to our crew as our permanent navigator. He flew his first one with us today.

Feb. 24, 1945

No. 18 today. An abortive because of bad weather. We brought our bombs back to base.

Feb. 28, 1945

Hit a bridge in the vital Brenner Pass today over which the Germans were trying to move troops from

He that respects himself is safe from others.—*Longfellow*

Italy to the Russian Front.
This was 19 for me. We
picked up a big flak
hole right between Bill
and I in the floor boards.
Too close for comfort.
Joe Herdman was shot down
on this raid. We're hoping
he is still alive even
though it would mean
he were a P.O.W.

march. 9, 1945

Got No. 20 today. a good
mission over the marshalling
yards at Wienner neustadt.
Flew No. 4 spot for the
fourth consecutive mission.
Think we plastered the
target

Going back to Dec. 18, 1944, my good friend Bob Sanderson ("Sandy") who was checking out a new crew crashed & was killed instantly at Ancona. He was hit badly over the target & tried to make it back to Ancona on two engines, but luck was against him. Sandy was a great boy & a fine pilot. I hated like everything to see him go.

Don Perry had to ditch in the adriatic sometime ago after running out of gas. His engineer broke his pelvis & his radio operator broke his leg, but no one was killed. Don received the D.F.C.

Men ought always to pray, and not to faint.
—Luke XVIII: 1

march 14, 1945

I came back from my 21st mission today to learn that I was the dad of a baby girl. This is about the best news I ever hope to receive. Marian and Eleanor are both doing fine. Now I really have to get home.

The mission was to Bruck but we hit the marshalling yds. at Wiener neutstadt because the weather was better there. Flew no. 4 spot again Major McCord led the group.

march 16, 1945

Amstteten, Austria marshalling yards was my 22nd target. Very smooth mission. We

Forewarned, forearmed; to be prepared is half the victory.—*Cervantes* had a good percentage of our bombs on the target.

March 19, 1945

No. 23 today. A bombing mission run off at 17,000 feet on a no flak target. We hit the marshalling yards at Muhldorf, Germany. We are trying to cut off German supplies moving to the Russian front. Again we plastered the target squarely. Flew "The Dakota Queen" (279) today for the first time since it was flown back from the Isle of Vis.

Sam Adams my original navigator has' been missing in action' since the Mar. 12th mission to Vienna. He was flying as a mickey man with Don Schultz a pilot from another sqdn. They were hit over the target & I went down between the Russian & German lines. The Russians killed the nose navigator thinking they were Germans using an American B-24. Von Shultz & his cofilot are back but they do not know where the rest of the crew including Sam are. We hope they are still alive.
— Joe Hordman's cofilot

returned from a partisan area near Pola where the crew bailed out after being hit on the Brenner Pass raid of Feb. 28th He says that Joe is probably a prisoner of war with several of the other fellows. One of them is believed to have been killed by the Fascists as he hung in his chute coming down.

mar. 21, 1945

Neuburg air drome, north of Munich, was our target today. It is reported that we hit this target with as great a destructive accuracy as any airdrome hit in this war. It was a jet field

The nation's honor is dearer than the nation's comfort.
—*Wilson*

longing the training program
for Germany's new Me-
262's. This was no. 24
for me.

Mar. 22, 1945
No. 25 today. An 8:40
haul to Kralupy oil Refinery
one of the last of Germany's
oil refineries. Were almost
hit by fighters today but
Jerry thought better when
he saw our escort. For
the third straight time we
landed with more gas left
than any other plane on
the field.

May. 25
Hit Prague Tank works
for no. 26 today.
This is the first

Worse than war is the fear of war.
—Seneca

time Prague has been hit since the war began. we really initiated them right. their gunners were rusty although they threw plenty of flak our way.

april 1, 1945

we bombed today from the lowest altitude yet — 14,000 feet. our target was the Krieglach R.R. bridge near Graz. we could see the Russians advancing below us near the target. This was no. 27 for me. we leave for rest camp at Capri and Rome tomorrow.

april 11, 1945

arrived back from Rome yesterday via a 454th plane.

We give up the fort when there's not a man left to defend it.—*Captain George Croghan*

Flew No. 28 today when we hit a bridge in the Brenner Pass. Too much accurate flak to suit me. We didn't drop on the bridge however as it was smoke obscured from the bombs of the preceding group. We picked an alternate at Roito, Italy. Hit a big fuel dump there.

April 15, 1945
No. 29 today was something new for the heavies. We hit the front line area around Bologna. Quite a tactical situation. The 5th army boys laid down a barrage for us to tie up as much ack

ack as possible, but Jerry still managed to make it plenty hot for us. We saw a lot of pink flak today. Looks like mountains of strawberry ice cream.

April 16, 1945

We tried to take another crack at Jerry's front line material today but the weather fooled us. The target was completely cloud covered, so we had to bring our bombs back to base. We got credit for the mission, however. Giving me no. 30.

April 17, 1945

Today made three in a row for me. No. 31 — another crack at the Bologna

The first requisite of a good citizen in this republic of ours is that he shall be able and willing to pull his own weight.—*T. Roosevelt*

area. The major really pulled a good piece of evasive action today. Only one ship was hit & he made it back to base O.K. We took a few light hits the 15th when we first hit Bologna but were untouched today.

April 18, 1945

Today made four in a row for me — all to the front lines in the Bologna area. The Fifth & Eighth armys should begin to move any day now as we are leveling everything ahead of them. This no. 32 for me.

April 23, 1945

No 33 today. Hit a vital road bridge at Padua to cut off one of Jerries escape routes from northern Italy

April 24, 1945

Hit an alternate target today — Ossoppo motor Transport Dept. We went over the primary but didn't drop our bombs as the target was smoke obscured. This was 34 for me.

April 25, 1945

Well that last one is now behind me. It was my toughest mission. We hit the Linz main station. Our ship # 34 was hit badly over the target.

Give me liberty, or give me death.
—*Patrick Henry*

It took a flak hit in his left thigh. All our hydraulic lines were cut hopelessly so to land we had to crank our gear down manually, pump the flaps down, & I then throw out parachute to stop us when we were on the ground. We ended up at the end of the runway O.K. with no further damage to the plane or the fellows. We had well over 75 holes in our plane — some of which were amazingly close to some of us. In a way this was a good one to quit on because

it made me more thankful
than ever that I had
finished.

May 8, 1945

The European war is
over. Everyone is drunk
but happy.

My last mission
also proved to be the
last one that the 15th
Air Force flew. Guess
I should consider myself
lucky not to have missed
that one enemy though
it did scare the devil
out of me.

Difficulties are things that show what men are.
—*Epictetus*

"Statesmen of the Lost Cause" Burton Hendrick
Civil war history of the southern side

Carbondale History text.

Learn to obey before you command.
—*Solon*

Glory is the true and honorable recompense of gallant
actions.—*Le Sage*

Transcript High School

Subjects	Units
English	4
Algebra	1
Geometry	1
Am. Hist	1
Civics	½
Soc. Probs.	½
Latin	2
Med. Hist.	1
Physics	1
Biology	1
Geog.	½
Cons. Prob	½
Manual Tng	1 ¾
Music	2 ¼
Non-solids	1 ¼
Total	19 ½

"Statesmen of the Lost Cause"
Burton J. Hendrick

I speak the password primeval, I give the sign of democracy.

Little, Brown, & Co.   Boston, Mass   Walt Whitman

College

Subjects	Whrs.	Qr. Hrs.	Grade
1940-41			
Psy, Gen. 101	12	3	A
Psy, Mental 104	12	2	A
English 101, 102	24	10	A A
Mus App. 110	12	5	A
Phys. Ed, Bskt 204	12	1	Credit
Prin. of Econ. 102	12	5	B
German, 102, 103	24	10	B C
Adv. Speech 203	12	5	A
Probs. Econ. 103	12	5	B
Phy. Ed, First aid 205	12	2	Cr.
Debate 311	12	(2)	A
Speech 411 Extemp & oratory	12	(2)	B
Phys. Ed.	24	2	Cr. Cr.
Chapel	36		Cls. Cr.
1941-42			
Adv. Sp. Comp. 304	12	5	A
Anc. Hist 201	12	5	A
Bus. Law 302	12	5	A
Arg. & Debate 202	12	5	A
Med. European Hist 202	12	5	A

Leave not a stain in thine honor.
—Ecclesiasticus XXXIII: 22

117

Pol. Science Am. Govt 216   12   5   A
Sur. of Am. Lit. 206   12   5   A
Hist. of Mod Europe 203   12   5   A
C P A   12   5   C
Sp. 311, 411 - Debate, Ept. Ord. 12 (4) A
Phys. Ed.   36   3   Cr. Cr.
Chapel   36   Cr. Cr. Cr.

                1942-43

College Algebra 102   12   5   A
Hist. of U.S. to 1865 - 301   12   5   A
Modern Philosophy 307   12   5   A
Sur. of Eng. Lit.   6   2.5 B
Speech 205 - Interp.   6   2.5 B
Hist of U.S. 1865-1940 302   6   5   A
Play Pro. 302   6   2.5 B
Speech 311 Debate   6   (1) A
Phys. Ed.   18 1.5 Cr. Cr.
Chapel   12   Cr.

Total Quarter Hours 136
Nine Hrs. in parenthesis for   29
(Such not to be counted toward)
grad   127

15 105 117½ 118

Freedom exists only where the people take care of the
government.—Woodrow Wilson " Civilization Past
History book used at Carbondale & Present

THE FOLKS BACK HOME

Name _____
Address _____
City _____ State _____

Name _____
Address _____
City _____ State _____

Name _____
Address _____
City _____ State _____

Name _____
Address _____
City _____ State _____

Name _____
Address _____
City _____ State _____

DATES TO REMEMBER

BIRTHDAYS, ANNIVERSARIES AND SPECIAL OCCASIONS I
WANT TO REMEMBER BY SENDING A GREETING OR GIFT

Feb. 3
Date
Mother
Name
Birthday
Occasion

Feb. 7
Date
Mildred
Name
Birthday
Occasion

April 11
Date
Dad
Name
Birthday
Occasion

June, 11
Date
Laurence
Name
Birthday
Occasion

Nov. 3
Date
Olive
Name
Birthday
Occasion

Nov. 25
Date
Cleavie & Ola
Name
Birthday
Occasion

Jan. 8
Date
Mother & Dad
Name
Wedding Anniversary
Occasion

Date
Name
Occasion

Date
Name
Occasion

Date
Name
Occasion

Date
Name
Occasion

Date
Name
Occasion

Date
Name
Occasion

Date
Name
Occasion

Date
Name
Occasion

Date
Name
Occasion

Date
Name
Occasion

Date
Name
Occasion

Date
Name
Occasion

Date
Name
Occasion

GIFTS
I HAVE RECEIVED
For Which I Want to Express Appreciation

GIFTS I HAVE RECEIVED

Gift _Scheaffer Life-time Pen_	Gift _Picture_
When Received _2-19-1943_	When Received
From Whom _Ruth & Ardith Rumbolz_	From Whom _Eleanor_
Gift _Flash-light_	Gift
When Received _2-19-1943_	When Received
From Whom _mrs. Irway_	From Whom
Gift _Toilet set with holder_	Gift
When Received _2-18-1943_	When Received
From Whom _mother_	From Whom
Gift _Stationary_	Gift
When Received _2-19-1943_	When Received
From Whom _Mr. & Mrs. Ledfort_	From Whom
Gift _one dollar bill_	Gift
When Received _2-19-1943_	When Received
From Whom _Mrs. Davison_	From Whom

GIFTS I HAVE RECEIVED

Gift	Gift
When Received	When Received
From Whom	From Whom
Gift	Gift
When Received	When Received
From Whom	From Whom
Gift	Gift
When Received	When Received
From Whom	From Whom
Gift	Gift
When Received	When Received
From Whom	From Whom
Gift	Gift
When Received	When Received
From Whom	From Whom
Gift	Gift
When Received	When Received
From Whom	From Whom
Gift	Gift
When Received	When Received
From Whom	From Whom

PLACES
I HAVE BEEN

DATE, DESCRIPTION, AND MY IMPRESSIONS OF
PLACES I WANT TO REMEMBER HAVING VISITED

Omaha, Neb.- 2-20-1943- was
impressed by the theatre and the
Union R.R. Station. Both were huge
and beautifully decorated.

Kansas City, Mo.- 2-20-1943.- We
went through here at night, but
was impressed by the city's lights
and the new war industries which
are operating day and night.

Memphis, Tenn.- enroute to
San Antonio.

New Orleans- enroute to
San Antonio.

Houston, Tex.- enroute to
San Antonio.

AUTOGRAPHS

Have Each of Your Buddies Write a Verse, Sentiment, or Characteristic Comment . . . and Sign His Name

★ ★ ★ ★ ★ ★ ★ ★ ★ ★ ★ ★ ★ ★ ★

"Pud" Mansfield
Lucas.
Kansas
Best of Luck George.
in anything you under-
take to do -- To another H.P. (Ha)

Signature Wilbur D. Mansfield

H. L. "Mac." McGraw
Sioux City,
Iowa
1845 So. Cedar

Keep the nose up and the
wings level and don't get
too hot -- the plane can't stand it.

Signature Harry L. McGraw

Stanley Meyers
7 Grinnan Place
Baldwin
New York

Good luck George!
you'll make the grade,
our country needs you.

Stanley Meyers
Signature

Richard L. Miller
9 Matthews Place
Brooklyn, N.Y.

The West is ok. for my money
and dont let us New Yorkers
get you.

Richard L. Miller
Signature

Joseph J. Linhart
2545 Valentine Ave
Bronx, New York

To a favorite son of Mitchell, S.D.
Its my good fortune to know
and associate with such a swell guy.

Joseph J. Linhart
Signature

George Lehren
215 Mt. Hope Pl
The Bronx, N.Y.

I know you'll make a fine
pilot & officer; you're too good
a man to be otherwise

George Lehren
Signature

Stanley J. Liedtke
Doniphin, Nebraska
RR #1

Best of Luck George but
keep the nose out of the
blue unless you like to fight

Stan Liedtke
Signature

Wilmer D. Landon
Russell, Kansas

I wish you a lot of luck
George. If you ever get to Kansas
drop in and see me.

Wilmer Landon
Signature

Jack R. Knicely
615 No. 34th
Omaha, Nebr.

Dear Mr. McGovern;
    Get on that laundry
detail - let's but! We're
dealing in tours - not gigs,
but tours.
    "Smilin" Jack Knicely
Signature

Charles Little
305 Univ Ave.
Hastings, Nebr.

Don't work too hard like
you and I at J B. Best
of luck.

    "Chuck" Little
Signature

124

Wallace W. Lake
Hebron, Nebr.

Keep 'Em Flying
George
Remember JB & GINU.
and take good care of
our girl. You lucky devil!

Wallace (Rocky) Lake
Signature

Alfred Francis "Jack" McEachen
Dodge City, Kansas

You may not have been
born in Kansas George,
but as one Westerner
to another you tops-lets
keep 'Em Flying.

Alfred F. "Jack" McEachen
Signature

Jack H. Lederman
2856 West 20 St.
Brooklyn N.Y.

I may be from
the big city (Coney Island)
but I'll always have to
"hut" to keep up with you,
my western friend.
(H.P.) Jack Henry Lederman
Signature

Richard W. Kruse
1302 So. 44 d St.
Omaha, Nebraska

We have had good
and bad times here in
carbondale together & I only
hope you continue as
well as you have here.
Dick Kruse
Signature

125

THOMAS H. JOYCE
3306 High Street
Des Moines, Iowa

I suppose George you're getting
use to the A.A.F. but kind of miss
furloughs like the army issues
well here's to classification and a
breeze through the whole course
Signature Thomas H. Joyce

James E. Bubb
#3 Maynard St
So. Williamsport, 17, Pa.

Lots of luck in everything.
Mac & it's been nice knowing
you. Stay right on the beam boy
and you'll make a "hot pilot"
Signature Jim Bubb.

Vincent J. Silvestri
1743 White Plains Rd.
N.Y.C., N.Y.

I've known few westerners in
my years of vast travel & experience
but upon seeing your gal's picture all
I can say is: "God Bless America - all of it!"
Signature Vincent J. Silvestri

Jack Nixon
290 East 205 St.
Bronx, N.Y. City

We're off to see the "wizard".
Drop into New York some time
and I'll show you a good town.
Tons of luck.
Signature John J. Nixon

126

Phillip E. Lyness
7240 Adams St.
Lincoln, Nebraska.

It's been swell to have
known you, George. Best of
luck along the way.

Phillip E. Lyness
Signature

Philip J. Wilkinson.

38-85 AVENUE
FLORAL PARK L.I.
NEW YORK

Best Wishes For success.
"I still like that picture"

Signature

Terrence C. Maloy
5313 6TH AVE
APT. 4D
Brooklyn, N.Y.

Work hard, try hard and all the
things you desire will become
real and true.

Terry Maloy
Signature

Signature

127

FIRST AID

The first aid measures here described are not intended to replace the aid and advice of a physician. They are suggested procedures to be used in emergencies. Accidents are acute emergencies; they require prompt, cool action in order to avoid catastrophe. The discussion that follows outlines several procedures which should prove beneficial until a doctor arrives.

In any accident, the most important considerations, in the order named are: (1) the control of excessive bleeding by stopping the rapid escape of blood from injured vessels; (2) the immediate institution of artificial respiration if breathing has ceased; (3) the combating of shock. The symptoms of shock are (1) pallor; (2) cold sweat; (3) dilated pupils; (4) weak and rapid pulse; (5) subnormal temperature; and (6) general weakness (tendency toward fainting). Effort should be made to reassure the patient concerning his condition. If possible, a badly injured person should not be moved, and injured parts of the body should not be handled unnecessarily. Normal body heat should be maintained by blankets and hot water bottles.

Artificial Respiration—This is employed whenever normal breathing has ceased. Cessation of breathing may be due to electric shock, suffocation from poisonous gases, or drowning (caused by water filling the upper air passages). The best known and most practical method is the Schaeffer Prone-Pressure method, which consists of the alternate application of pressure to force air out of the lungs and release of pressure to draw air into the lungs. Before applying this treatment, false teeth, chewing gum, or any foreign substance should be removed from the mouth. The patient should be placed face down with his head turned to one side and resting on his hand. The tongue should be drawn forward and to one side of the mouth. If there is water in the air passages, the patient should be lifted with hands placed under his abdomen, so that whatever water is present may drain out. But this should all be done very quickly, as seconds may mean the life of the patient. It is impor-

tant to keep the jaws open. The operator should kneel astride the patient's knees, place the palms of the hands upon the back of the lower chest region, and gradually but firmly exert pressure forward and downward; then remove the hands quickly. The pressing and releasing should be rhythmic, about 12 times a minute, giving 5 seconds for the double movement of compression and sudden relaxation. Artificial respiration should be continued for as much as 6 hours or more if the patient does not resume normal breathing sooner.

Burns and Scalds—As there is no essential difference between burns and scalds, the treatment of them is the same. The fundamental principle in the treatment of burns is the prevention of infection. Burned tissues are devitalized and are more apt to become infected than normal tissue. Infection constitutes a threat to life and even if overcome, results in unsightly scars and crippling deformities. Cleanliness, therefore, is the simplest and most effective measure in the treatment of burns. Burned surfaces should be washed with soap and water and should be covered with a dry sterile bandage. Severe burns cause shock, the treatment of which is the most important first aid measure in such conditions.

In treating burns caused by strong acids or alkalies the caustic agent should first be removed by gently washing with water. Baking soda may then be employed for neutralizing a burn of either type.

Cuts—These are dangerous for two chief reasons: (1) They cause a loss of blood, which might be very serious; or (2) they may introduce infection into the blood stream. Virulent and deadly germs, present in the air and on the skin, need only the tiniest opening imaginable to penetrate the skin and cause a severe illness and even death. In treating small cuts where bleeding is not profuse, the most important consideration is the prevention of infection. For this reason bleeding should be allowed, so that any germs that have entered the opening may be carried away by the flow of blood. After the wound has bled for a short while, it should be thoroughly cleansed with soap and water. Small cuts usually stop bleeding of themselves.

In the treatment of large cuts, however, the most important consideration is the prevention of the loss of blood. Direct pressure upon the bleeding point is the most valuable single measure in the control of bleeding. Pressure should be applied continuously until the bleeding has stopped and a clot of blood formed. Elevation of the wounded part will also help, because in this way the blood pressure in the part is reduced and clotting is facilitated. Tourniquets have been much advertised and much abused. The commonest errors are in too loose an application, which still permits bleeding, and in too tight or too long an application, which injures tissues and deprives them of their vital blood supply. Their use should be limited to those accidents which involve the severance of large arteries. In that case anything like a belt, cord, rope, or piece of clothing may be twisted above the bleeding point and tightened up until the bleeding stops. It is always advisable to release the tourniquet at least every fifteen minutes in order to flush the parts below it with blood, and thus help to prevent a complication like gangrene.

After the flow of blood has been stopped, the area around the wound should be cleansed with soap and water, and any foreign matter such as dirt should be removed from the wound. The person administering first aid should make sure that his own hands are rendered clean by thoroughly scrubbing them with soap and water.

Dislocation—When the strain producing a sprain does more than stretch the ligament by tearing it, there is a dislocation of the joint, evidenced by the change in shape, by pain, and by swelling. Hot towels should be applied, the patient placed in a comfortable position, and the doctor summoned.

Sprains are partial or complete tears of supporting ligaments of a joint, due to excessive motion in some direction. It is very difficult even for a physician to differentiate between a severe sprain and a possible fracture; X-ray may be necessary. However, before the doctor arrives, it is advisable to place the joint in the most comfortable position and elevate the injured part as high as possible. A light pressure with a snug but comfortably-fitting bandage may be applied. The bandage should be kept wet with cold applications of water for the first few hours; then with hot water.

Fractures—The first aid that a fracture receives may determine its healing results. There is no need of haste to transport the patient somewhere. The first thing to consider is the treatment of the shock which is present in almost all cases of fractures. The patient must be kept warm; stimulants may be administered. Clean and sterile dressings should be applied to compound fractures (fractures in which bone fragments project through the skin), but no attempt should be made

to reduce or manipulate the fracture in any manner. Most important of all is to splint the injured member with four points of fixation—two above and two below the fracture. After the splint is adjusted, the patient may be moved (in a horizontal position) and any unnecessary jarring should be avoided.

Heat Prostration or Heat Stroke—This occurs in tropics or zones in which there has been a long-continued heat wave. It is brought on by ill health, intemperance, a susceptibility to heat, or because of previous attacks. The attacks start with faintness, dizziness, headache, nausea, and difficulty in walking. The skin becomes pale, cold, and moist; the pulse becomes rapid though weak; breathing is very rapid; and the pupils of the eyes become dilated. The victim should at once be placed in a recumbent position and cold towels applied to his head. If his temperature has dropped below normal he should be kept warm with blankets and hot water bottles applied to his body. Stimulants such as aromatic spirits of ammonia may be used by inhalation. Nothing should be given by mouth until the victim is fully conscious.

Sunstroke—This is brought on by continued exposure to bright sunlight. The first signs of impending sunstroke are dizziness, dry skin, headache, weakness, and rapid breathing. Shortly afterward there is intense thirst, restlessness, flushed face, rapid pulse, throbbing of arteries in face and neck, and twitching of the muscles all over the body. The patient should immediately be taken out of the heat to a cool place, his clothing loosened, and cold compresses applied to the head, neck, and chest. The rest of the body should be continuously fanned and sponged with cold water. The head should be kept high and cooled. A little cold salt water may be administered internally.

Nose Bleed—The causes of nose bleeds are numerous. Most frequently they are caused by blows upon the nose, by scratching the nose to remove dried secretions, by high blood pressure, and by fractures at the base of the skull. Most nose bleeds cease spontaneously; therefore it is best to keep the patient quiet. The upright position of the patient lowers the blood pressure and favors clotting. The patient should be directed to breathe quietly through the mouth, in order not to loosen the clots. The nose should not be blown. Time honored remedies such as placing ice on the back of the neck are of value chiefly in that they keep the patient quiet and in an upright position. Repeated or uncontrollable hemorrhage demands a physician's care.

MY DISCHARGE

FROM THE SERVICE

DATE ....

PLACE ....

RANK ....

COMMENT ....

....

....

....

....

....

....

★ ★ ★ ★ ★ ★ ★ ★ ★ ★ ★ ★ ★ ★ ★ ★

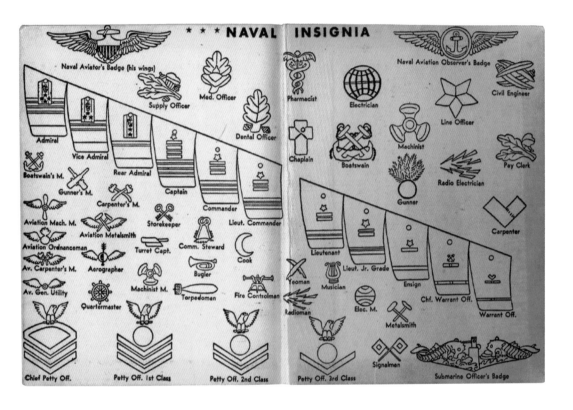

★ ★ ★ NAVAL INSIGNIA

Naval Aviator's Badge (his wings)

Supply Officer

Med. Officer

Dental Officer

Admiral

Vice Admiral

Rear Admiral

Captain

Commander

Lieut. Commander

Boatswain's M.

Gunner's M.

Carpenter's M.

Storekeeper

Aviation Mach. M.

Aviation Metalsmith

Aviation Ordnanceman

Turret Capt.

Comm. Steward

Cook

Av. Carpenter's M.

Aerographer

Bugler

Av. Gen. Utility

Quartermaster

Machinist M.

Torpedoman

Fire Controlman

Chief Petty Off.

Petty Off. 1st Class

Petty Off. 2nd Class

Pharmacist

Electrician

Naval Aviation Observer's Badge

Civil Engineer

Line Officer

Chaplain

Boatswain

Machinist

Pay Clerk

Gunner

Radio Electrician

Carpenter

Lieutenant

Lieut. Jr. Grade

Ensign

Chf. Warrant Off.

Warrant Off.

Yeoman

Musician

Radioman

Elec. M.

Metalsmith

Signalmen

Submarine Officer's Badge

Petty Off. 3rd Class

131

Our train was scheduled to leave Mitchell at 8 P.M. on Feb. 19, 1943. We were delayed about an hour and a half, but spent the time visiting with students and faculty members from the college who came down to see us off. Most of my close friends, my family, and the twins were there.

On the sleeper to Omaha we met a couple of air cadets who were going to Omaha with Kreiman and I. We pulled into Omaha about 10 A.M. Sat. Feb. 20.

At the induction center in Omaha we met Sgt. Francis Robbins whom we ate dinner with. He gave us some of the inside dope which every man in the army seems to know. By the way the first lesson I learned in the army is that it's best to ignore all rumors and the so-called inside dope.

We spent the afternoon in Omaha at Nebraska's largest theater - it was really beautiful. The feature attraction was a stage show by Chico Marx and his orchestra. We got a bang out of it.

At 4 P.M. we got onto a troop train with 250 other air cadets - all bound for Jefferson Barracks, MO. In spite of the fact that it took us until 6 A.M. the next day to get to J.B. and we neither slept nor ate during this trip, I really enjoyed it. The fellows were all in a good mood. I was told and it was easily apparent that we had the cream of the crop in our outfit. We were all college men - mostly juniors and seniors. Walt and I met two fellows whom we got to know fairly well on the train - Russ Heikes from Vermillion and Chuck Burke from Pierre.

Upon our arrival at J.B. we were led to the general mess hall for a top-notch breakfast which really hit the spot. Everywhere we went in the camp we heard the cry "You won't like it here."

It seems that due to the wet, changing weather nearly everyone had a bad cold. Hundreds of the fellows were down with pneumonia - many had died. We resolved to be careful. The old veterans claim it'll get you, anyway.

We were then assigned to our huts - ten men to each hut. Walt Kreiman & I who had stuck together since leaving Mitchell both managed to get in the same hut - in fact the same double bunk. He in the upper berth. I in the lower.

After getting our blankets, we learned how to make up an army bunk. Every fold must be just so, or K.P. is the result. Also the hut must be left in perfect order, or we are deprived of our passes into St. Louis. That was our second lesson - the army is precise and exacting. Everything is done according to army methods.

I also discovered that in the army everybody gripes about everything from the weather to the food. It's just the soldiers way of relaxing and getting rid of tension. As yet we have had nothing to gripe about. Our "Sarg". is O.K. He's more lenient than most of them.

We met Bob Mackey this evening, and some other fellows from Mitchell. Red Fuller lives across the street from our hut; so we have plenty of company. It makes it easier to start out with fellows you know. All the boys are friendly, though, and it's easy to get acquainted. We've got some A-1 fellows in our hut. One of them is married.

After writing a few letters we turned in and the first day in camp was over. In spite of the continuous cry "You won't like it here," we enjoyed the first day thoroughly. Here's hoping it won't get any worse, but it probably will. They tell us we are really in earnest about this war.

Mar. 2, 1943

After 10 days at J.B. we find that it is getting easier for us all the time as we learn some of the tricks and methods of the army. We have sore arms from our first 3 shots for vaccinations. Received a card from Bob Mackey who has been transferred to Coe College, Iowa. We hope soon to join him.

Those letters from home are really helping a lot - especially the love letters. Mail is more valuable than food in the army.

We had the day off because of a snow storm which made it impossible to drill. Our swell sergeant got us out of detail work by a few white lies to the top sergeant.

We had our first real inspection of huts and lockers today and passed with flying colors.

Well, we are all nursing some very sore arms tonight having received our second vaccinations today. We also passed our second real inspection. Yesterday we were confined to our area because some hut in our Flight C wasn't clean, but we are out again tonight. Six of the boys in our platoon 1504 were shipped out today. The rest of us are anxiously hoping for the day when we will get our shipping orders. Dick Nash, hut mate, included in 6

We have completed all our drill maneuvers and now it is simply a matter of practice until we become proficient. Got my daily letter from Eleanor. How I wait for her mail and the other mail from home. Wrote a lot of letters myself the last few days.

Today we got something that all of us have been hoping for - shipping orders. Our whole flight except for the sick boys is to leave tomorrow. Rumors are flying thick and fast as to where we are going. Some say West Virginia, others Illinois, still others Wisconsin. At any rate we are all glad to be going. Our month of training at Jefferson Barracks has been very valuable, but also very hard and sometimes discouraging. Most of us had bad colds or other ills while we were here. Due to the location of the camp on the Mississippi River just at the south edge of St. Louis it is damp here and disease spreads easily.

To list some of the things we have done at J.B. I could mention the following things: First of all we learned a lot about drilling. Sergeant Trumbs is a very good drill man and he succeeded in making us one of the best drill platoons on the post.

Secondly we learned to fire an army Springfield rifle. Our first day on the rifle range was perhaps one of our most enjoyable days at J.B. We also were given a chance to fire a clip in the army's Thompsen Sub-Machine Gun. I myself, was to excited to be very accurate with the piece, but better luck next time.

Gas mask drill - another event at J.B. After being carefully instructed in the use of the gas mask we were marched over to the gas chamber and subjected to 15 minutes of tear gas. Then we took off our masks for 30 seconds to get a "taste" of tear gas. Needless to say we were all crying for the next half hour. At least we had learned to appreciate the army's gas mask - the finest in the world.

One of our most interesting drills at J.B. was bayonet practice. Using wooden guns we were taught and practiced thrusts, jabs, vertical and horizontal butt kicks and smashes, and other bayonet tactics. This is one type of fighting I think would be worse than any other. After bayonet practice, two of the boys in our platoon showed us a little jiu jitsi. I managed to pick up a few holds that I think may be useful some day.

We also mastered the manual of arms which is the various positions and movements of the rifle.

After going over to medical four times for typhoid, small pox and tetanus shots our arms were pretty well poked full of holes. We now feel fairly well protected against about every disease imaginable.

After two weeks of processing we were given passes into St. Louis any day of the week. I managed to get in several times before we left. Walt Kreiman and I heard the St. Louis Symphony with Arthur Rubenstein at the piano. He was very good. The high light of the entertainment in St. Louis, however, was a concert by Marian Anderson. We service men and women were all seated behind Miss Anderson on the stage - a great honor we thought. She turned around and sang several numbers to us and the audience applauded loudly. The concert was marvelous. Probably the best music I have ever heard. I succeeded in getting Miss Anderson's autograph which I sent to Olive.

I shall never forget the fine facilities of the U.S.O. Center in St. Louis. They have everything for the soldiers enjoyment. We could take showers, press our clothes, shave, play ping pong, play the piano, read, write letters, make phone calls, get invitations to private homes, play games or almost anything imaginable. If we so wished there were hostesses for everyone who wanted company.

St. Louis is the eigth largest city in the U.S. and I imagine one of the oldest. It has several beautiful parks. I visited Forest Park and Shaws Gardens - two of the most beautiful places in the world.

This then, has been some of things that took up our time at Jefferson

Barracks. It has been a very busy eventful month. Those were awfully long days from 5 A.M. to 9 P.M. every day of the week. It has been good for us, though, especially the housemaid duties. Incidentally I almost forgot to mention K.P. I spent this much dreaded day taking trays full of dishes from a steam dish washer. It was really a tough day. One that I'll always remember.

I must not forget to mention guard duty. This wasn't so bad. I had the watch from 2 to 4 A.M. Only the novelty of the job for excitement on my post.

And now a little description of our huts. At first there were ten of us to a hut but later only eight. The huts were rude wooden structures about eighteen by eighteen feet. There was no furniture in the room except our bunks and our lockers. These huts were hard to keep clean; so we had to mop them or G.J. them every morning. It was really a sight to see us all pushing mops at 5 A.M. in the morning. We also had to keep a fire in our stoves at all the times as the huts were full of cracks and the air was chilling and damp.

My first hut mates were the following boys: Laird Loomis, U. of Missouri; Leslie Livingston, U. of Neb.; Darrell Ludi, U. of Neb.; Dick Nash, U. of Neb.; Homer Livermore, Uni. of Neb.; Bill Lowery, Uni. of Neb.; Bill Lukely, Creighton Uni.; Walter Kreiman, D.W.U. I lived with these boys for two weeks. The second two weeks were spent with these boys (colleges follow names): Chuck Little, Hastings College; Don Linnaman, Peru College; (cont.) Wallace "Rocky" Lake, Hastings Col.; Percy Kirkeley, Augustana; Don Lee, Iowa State College; Dave Lescher, Midland College; and one of the old hut mates Homer Livermore, Uni. of Neb. A few days before we left J.B. Homer was taken sick and had to go to the hospital. He was still there when we were leaving. My first hut mates were very congenial and we got along fine, but the next fellows were hard to get along with. All in all we managed pretty well, however.

This then completes the story of a month at Jefferson Barracks. It has been good training, but we are are all heaving a sigh of relief that it is in the past.

Well, one of the rumors was right. We are in Carbondale, Illinois. We arrived here on Tuesday. This college is Southern Illinois State Normal University. It is a beautiful old college and campus. Seems heavenly compared to old J.B. First, however, a word about our trip down here. We first clambered into a fleet of army trucks like a bunch of excited kids and were whisked down to the shipping depot. There we were given "short arm" inspections while everyone held his breath for fear he had a temperature. A temperature meant being scratched from the shipping list - too bad for a few boys.

After passing inspection we were loaded onto a very crowded troop train and taken into St. Louis. From there we transferred to a larger and far better train and came directly to Carbondale arriving about 5 P.M.

So far life here has been rather monotonous for me as I have been confined to quarantine because of a pleuresy in the region around my left eye. It is better today so I hope to be on the go again tomorrow. I can see that the military discipline is going to be more than strict here. It is almost unbelievable to see how rigid they are in enforcing the thousand and one military rules here. We must even watch at attention in the halls and on the campus. We can eat only with our right hand, etc.

My room-mate is busy polishing our brass door knocks for inspection. Maybe this idea of reporting for sick call isn't so bad after all. It's pretty convenient to have orders to stay in bed while your buddy does your work for you. I'd still like to be up, however,

Last night a box of home made fudge came in from Eleanor and Mildred. Gee is it ever good. I'd like to kiss them both for it, but then that will have to wait. By the way, it would really be nice to be home for awhile. I'm slightly homesick today. Wish I could see Eleanor and my mother for awhile. Sent them a telegram last night. My roommate from J.B. and Nebraska University, Bill Lowery wrote Eleanor a letter for me last night as my eye was bothering me.

June 12, 1943

Today everyone in Flight D is rejoicing. After three months of hitting the books we begin to fly. Today we moved back to old Anthony Hall from University Courts. Bill and I still managed to be room-mates. Walt Kreiman and his group having completed their required 10 hours of flying left for San Antonio today. Bill & I have his old room.

June 26, 1943

Finished ten hours of flying that we are to get in Carbondale. I had forgotten nearly all that I knew about flying in the time since I took CPT. At the end of the ten hours though I felt capable of taking "her" up and landing alone. No solo flight here though. We'll have to wait until later for that. Looks as though our remaining two weeks in Carbondale at S.I.N.U. will be spent pretty much at ease. Only three classes a day. We sleep all morning.

Jumping back a month to May 28, 1943 I must record my first army furlough. After getting a letter from mother saying that dad was quite low I was given a ten day furlough. Nothing ever made me happier than a chance to go home for awhile. It seemed to me that the train for Mitchell never would get there although in reality we made very good time. I rode the Hiawatha from Chicago into Sioux Falls and hitch-hiked from there to Mitchell in the middle of the night - Foolish but the only thing I could do to get home as soon as I wanted to. The week at home was a dream but I came back with soaring spirits and a new drive to work. Wish the air corps could give more furloughs. I was especially glad to get home because the blood transfusion that I gave to dad seemed to help him.

July 10, 1943

At 2 A.M. this morning we left Carbondale for San Antonio. I spent my last evening in Carbondale visiting Cromeous and Dr. Harvey. They were very good to me during my stay at S.I.N.U. and did a lot to make me enjoy life at Carbondale. It was hard to say goodbye to these swell people and and the friendly spirit of Carbondale. The town had very few entertainment facilities but the hospitality of the people more than made up for that. I was invited out to dinner six or seven different Sundays to various church homes. The meals were wonderful and the friendliness of the people is the greater than any place I've ever been. Some day I'd like to go back to this little town in southern Illinois and visit the people who treated us so swell and the old college where we spent what will probably be our three and a half happiest months in the army. The faculty was not too strong, but our military and physical training program was of the best.

July 11, 1943

Deep in the heart of Texas. We arrived here about 430 this afternoon after an enjoyable trip. It's hard to believe but the army actually arranged sleepers for us on this trip. We came by way of Memphis and New Orleans which made it possible for me to go through four states I had never been in before. We were in New Orleans and Memphis each for a couple of hours, but had very little chance to see the towns. Most of the boys had their first experience of being propositioned by negroe chippies in New Orleans.

July 14, 1943

Today we started our classification to determine whether we will be a pilot, a navigator, or a bombardier. We took the seven hour mental test today under enough pressure to put some fellows on their backs.

The next day we got our psychomotor test which tests our coordination and reaction time. We are run through a series of all different kinds of weird looking machines which help to determine whether or not we have the stuff to become air crew members.

Following this comes the air corps famous no. 64 physical in which they go over us from head to toe. Only a perfect physical specimen can get through this maze of doctors and apparati. Needless to say I'm praying that I'll get through. The sinus trouble which I developed at J.B. may cause me some trouble.

There are four of us here in our barracks from Carbondale - Bill Lowery, Wilmer Landon, Fred Kirk and myself. We are in a barracks right next to the orderly room but that doesn't prevent us from using this classification period as an ideal time to gold brick for about 3 weeks.

Aug 1, 1943

Finally got to pre flight after being classified as a pilot. Seems like a great place but the discipline is terriffic.

Oct 1, 1943

Arrived in Muskogee for primary. We are now real pilots.

Oct. 16, 1943

My first solo flight as an army pilot - a day I'll never forget. This is the thing I've been dreaming about for a long time. I can now don the wings of a solo pilot.

Oct 27, 1943

Just passed my 20 hour progress check ride given to me by flight commander Dixson. It's a relief to know I was able to get by the check boss. Check rides are tough as a good percentage of our boys can testify who washed out on them.

Dec. 6, 1943

Arrived at Coffeyville, Kansas for basic. This place is a far cry from the modern barracks and country club atmosphere of primary. It seems to be taken for granted that basic will be rough.

Feb. 8, 1944

Basic is over. Wasn't as tough as we prophesied, but we've learned a lot about flying in the past nine weeks. Eleanor and Nell Perry left last night to drive to Pampa, Texas where we are going for advanced.

Feb. 9, 1944

We left Coffeyville on Pullmans last night arriving in Pampa this morning. From all reports it is liable to be pretty tough going for awhile here. Realizing that we'll be through in nine weeks, however, will keep morale high no matter how tough it gets.

April 15, 1944

Wings & commission at last. Now for an eleven day delay enroute before reporting to Liberal, Kansas for B-24 transition beginning April 27.

June 9, 1944 - Finished transition and flew to Lincoln, Nebraska today. Will be assigned a crew here.

June 25, '44 - Drove to Mt. Howe, Idaho with Don & Nell Perry and Joe Herdman. Ready now for the real combat training.

Sept. 17 - 1944 - Finished all three phases of combat training with my crew at Mt. Howe. We graduated today and will leave tomorrow for Topeka, Kans. for overseas assignments and a possible flyaway.

Oct 1, 1944 - We spent about a week at Topeka including a four day pass which Eleanor spent with me. We stayed as the Kansan Hotel as did the Round's. Met Commander Standish Hall and his wife who are Witchita friends of the Rounds. Mr. Rounds put on a wonderful crew banquet for us at the Kansan.

There were 41 crews in our group of which 30 were sent immediately to a P.O.E. for embarkation. The remaining 11 of us are now on our way to Langley Field, Va. to get our overseas assignment there. Why the move, we don't know.

Oct. 5, 1944 - We didn't get a flyaway at Langley, but merely wasted about five days there. Russ Greer, Sparks, Blanton, Sanderson and some of the others in our group did get flyaways but the last three on the list who were Joe Herdman, Don Perry, and myself are going over by boat. We moved to Camp Patrick Henry today - a camp just about 20 miles from Langley Field.

Oct. 13, 1944 - We boarded our ship tonight at Hampton Roads P.O.E. near Newport News.

Oct. 14, 1944 - We slipped out of port early this morning, but after spending the day joining with other ships to form a convoy we find ourselves just a few miles off shore from where we left and we don't port out to sea for good until about 8 P.M. this evening. The convoy seems to be moving southward to pick up still more ships.

Oct. 25, 1944 - This forenoon we passed through the strait of Gibraltar. It was a bright clear day and we had a good view of Gibraltar on our left and Africa on our right. We are now following a route along the coast of Africa. Our destination was announced several days ago as Naples, Italy but nevertheless we are holding close to the North African coast of the Mediterranean.

Oct 26, 1944 - Still flowing along the North African coastline. It is a continuous line of rugged mountainous country along the coast and has been in view ever since we entered the Mediterranean yesterday morning. We still have our convoy of about 25 ships - mostly cargo ships, tankers, troop ships and two or three escorting destroyers. We picked up some of these ships several days out at sea. All of the ships including ours are armed even though it is light armament. We are armed with a couple of 75 millimeter guns, and a group of 20 millimeters scattered from stern to stern. Occasionally a protective blimp or a naval patrol plane checks up to see that we are O.K. or perhaps just to add a little interest to their monotonous patrols.

Landed in Naples harbor today. Saw Ilse of Capri & Mt. Vesuvius coming in. Will spend tonight on board ship. Move to classification and shipping center tomorrow morning.

Moved to classification base near Caserta, Italy and Naples. Had our first experience in sleeping under a tent during Italy's well known rainy season.

Visited Caserta and Naples. People seem rather aimless and defeated looking. American cigarettes will buy almost anything.

Arrived at Bari, Italy today. Seems like a nice place.

We were taken by trucks today to our permanent squadrons. It rained all day and to make matters worse there was no tent for us. We found an old tent which we put up ourselves. The nights here are plenty cold and damp so I imagine we'll work on a stove tomorrow.

This squadron is reorganizing and as usual we came into it at the wrong time. The Italians have been hired to build a rock and cement floor for our tents. We do the rest. Namely, build stoves, chairs, tables, washstands and anything else to make life enjoyable here. We have succeeded in bartering with the Italians for such things as lamps, floor matts, dishes, etc.

Flew a formation practice mission today with a copilot named Kelleher.

Weather forced us to land at another base where I learned that the entire flight I flew with at Mt. Howe are here in the 15th. I saw Sandy and several of my other buddies.

Nov.

We have a system here whereby each pilot must fly five combat missions with an experienced crew before he can go out with his own crew. I had my first one today with Lt. Moreman's crew. Weather kept us from getting clear into the target, but because of the difficulty we encountered with the weather those of us who stuck with the formation were given credit for the mission. Our wing lost ten ships because of the severe icing and rough weather encountered. It was worse than flak. Target was Linz, Germany

Nov. 16, 1944

Started out today for Munich, my second mission, but we had to turn back because of a defective turbo. Lt. Bone's crew was the one I flew with today.

Nov. 17, 1944

Got credit for no. 2 today. We were scheduled to hit the no. 1 target of importance in Europe which is the huge oil refinery at Blechhammer, Germany. This is a heavily defended target and the flak is usually plenty rough. We were held up again by the weather though and had to bomb our secondary target which was the railroad yards at Gyor, Hungary. I flew with Lt. Asa's crew today. Flak wasn't too bad.

Nov. 18, 1944

No. 3. today. We really did a job today. Plastered the large German airfield at Vicenza, Italy. Nothing was left of the runways or the installations when we left. We also caught a lot of planes parked on the airfield. I flew with Lt. Armellino who was a buddy of mine at C.T.D. in Carbondale, Ill.

No. 4 - I feel guilty taking credit for this mission today. We couldn't find the target; so came back with all our bombs. There was a heavy undercast over the target and the radar ship was unable to pick up the target beneath it. The target was a large heavily defended locomotive works at Verona, Italy. Flew with Asa again today.

Completed no. 5 today. Again with Asa's crew. That means I can take up my own crew the next time and for the remaining thirty missions. Ralph has picked up four missions all with Lt. Moreman and Sam has one with Lt. Surbeck. The rest of the crew have no missions. They are ready to go now, however, as they were checked out on a practice gunnery mission today.

Again today the weather stopped us from reaching Blechhammer. We hit a rubber factory at Zlin Czechoslovakia - a town about 80 miles short of our intended target. One of Asa's gunners finished his missions off today and got the usual grease job by the ground crew.

Flew a practice mission with my own crew today. Have been playing touch football in the afternoons lately. It's our main recreation here.

Same old story. We didn't hit our target - again because of the weather. We were supposed to hit Graz, Austria - the railroad yards. This would have taken a lot of pressure off the Yugoslavs and the Russians because it is a funnel for supplies to the Germans in Yugo. We got credit for the mission - my sixth - because we were over enemy territory so long and encountered such rough weather. Our flight leader got separated from the main formation and took us down through some bad clouds over the Adriatic. Trying to stay in formation on instruments without being able to see who you're following is no fun. It scared me worse than any flak I've seen yet. Incidentally I haven't encountered much flak yet and no enemy fighters. Our bombardier today was McGahran.

Dec. 9, 1944

Knocked off no. 7 today. We've been trying desperately to get through bad weather these past few days but again today we failed to make it. The formation turned back at the head of the Adriatic when we ran up against a wall of clouds 30,000 feet and higher over Germany. Our crew had a little excitement today. We were flying 166, an old baby that had seen it's best days long ago. Just before the formation turned back we lost an engine - no. 3 - because of a cracked cylinder. I feathered the engine when the oil pressure fell off. We couldn't hold altitude nor stay with the formation. To make matters worse the weather had built up behind us so that I found myself in the soup and losing altitude on three engines with no. 1 also throwing oil badly. Our heaters were inoperative and we had been bitterly cold but needless to say I soon warmed up in all the hub bub. At first I decided to head for an emergency landing strip in northern Italy, but after descending on instruments through the soup to 12,000 feet no. 1 engine started running smoothly, and also we had lightened our load by throwing out our ammunition and dumping our bombs. I was able to hold altitude O.K. so decided to continue on the three good engines with the hope that no. 1 would hold out O.K. If it hadn't I knew we might very well have to leave the crate; so my navigator gave me a heading that kept us close to the coast at all times. We didn't relish the idea of an ice bath in the Adriatic. At any rate everything turned out O.K. I believe we learned more on this mission than anyone we have had yet.

Culver was our bombardier. This was his last mission. Our target was to have been the synthetic oil refinery at Moosebierbaum

Dec. 13, 1944

Received the news of dad's death today. He died Dec. 4th according to the cable which took almost ten days to reach me. The news hit me pretty hard and came as a shock to me even though I knew Dad was not well. I do know that he lived a beautiful life and died gloriously which is a great comfort now. He was the best man I ever knew and a wonderful dad. We'll miss him in a hundred ways, but he is happier now than ever before so we should not mourn his death too much.

Dec. 15, 1944

The mission which we had listed as no. 7 was taken away from us today because wing headquarters decided that we did not get close enough to the target to get credit for the mission.

We officially got no. 7 today though. Our target was the R.R. Yards at Linz, Austria. Col. Reefer led the wing. Our plane flew on his left wing in no. 3 spot. We had 917 today. Not a bad ship but very stiff to handle so Ralph and I felt we had done a days work by the time we landed. Our bombardier was Duncan. I believe we did a good job over the target although the target was overcast. The mickey ship was able to get a fairly good scope of the target.

Dec. 16, 1944

Our target today - no. 8 - was one of the roughest targets in Europe - the synthetic oil refinery at Brux. It has over 250 flak guns concentrated in the oil refinery area which is the thickest flak in Europe. The air force is concentrating now on knocking out these synthetic oil plants because it is the very life blood of Germany's war machine. The terrific oil shortage in Germany has kept their planes grounded and their mechanized army at a much slower pace than would have been the case if they had plenty of oil. I flew no. 3 spot again today on Col. Thayer's wing. My copilot today was a new man who is being checked out - Lt. Brown. The bombardier was McGahran. We flew 279 today.

Dec. 17, 1944

Another oil refinery today - the one at Oswiecim and Odertal in the Blechhammer flak area. This makes nine missions for me. We really got this one the hard way. On our takeoff today we had a tire blow out - the right main gear tire, but it went out after we cleared the field or rather just as we left the field. We went on to the target knowing that we had a rough landing and perhaps a crack up waiting for us on our return. While going to the target we lost our manifold pressure on no. 2 engine but pulled enough power on the other three to go into the target and get back. The air force lost ten ships to fighters and several to flak but we came through without a scratch. When we got back to the base I had everybody but the copilot, the engineer, and myself go back to the waist and brace themselves for the landing. We made sure that all the loose objects were tied down securely. As soon as we touched the runway I chopped the throttle on the side of the good wheel and advanced the throttle on the side of the blown tire at the same time holding down the left brake. We made the landing O.K. without damaging the plane in the least. Needless to say old terra firma felt plenty good. My copilot today was Lt. Brown and the bombardier was Lt. McGrahan. These two boys and Sam recommended me for the D.F.C. because of the landing but I don't feel as though I deserve a medal as yet.

Dec. 18, '44

Oswiecim oil refinery today for no. 10. My copilot today - another new pilot was Arendt. The bombardier McGahran. We flew 26 (974) today. The mission went off quite smoothly. No one was lost to flak or fighters. Flew no. 3 again today. Looks as though that spot is reserved for me. We hit Sopron, Austria instead of Oswiecim due to bad weather.

Dec. 20, 1944

I worked up a good sweat again today. We had another rough one - again in 279, the same ship that landed on one wheel two days ago. Our target today was Brux, but I lost an engine short of the target. We had no sooner started for home than I lost no. 3 engine and could not feather it. The first engine no. 2 came came back in partially after we came down from altitude but in the meantime no. 3 had caught fire. It continued to windmill until it froze up. I could hold altitude but couldn't depend on no. 2 which was running rough. In addition to that we were low on fuel and the weather was bad. We had a 1500 foot ceiling and it was so hazy that the navigator could hardly help me at all. Sam was not with me and the navigator Lt. Vince apparently was unable to do much of anything. Ralph contacted "Big Fence" and they gave us a heading to the Isle of Viz - a little island near the eastern side of the Adriatic. We finally found the island and located the landing strip. It is a British fighter strip and too short for a heavy bomber to land on, but we made it O.K. by the grace of God. A C-47 which was taking off saw us coming in; so they waited for us to land and then brought us back to our base.

We lost several planes and crews today in crash landings due to the shortage of fuel and bad weather. One of them is still unaccounted for. This makes no. 11 for me.

Dec. 25, 1944

After briefing for four straight days and not being able to get off because of bad weather we finally made it today. The air force wanted to do everything possible to give the Jerries a good plastering on Christmas; so we took off in spite of rain, muddy runways, and a ceiling of about 200 feet. We flew out over the Adriatic in a column of ships stacked down entrail of the lead ship. The ceiling gradually raised as we headed north to our rendezvous point at Vis. Major Welch was leading the group and to our disappointment he turned around at the head of the Adriatic and came home because two of our boxes failed to make the rendezvous. I couldn't see his point and we hated like the dickens to miss getting credit for the mission after working so hard to get through the weather. Our target was to have been Brux.

Dec. 26, 1944

Knocked off no. 12 today. The 15th Air Force is pledged to knock out Germany's synthetic oil production now that the loss of Ploestic has deprived her of the natural oil. We have already hit oil refineries at Brux, Odertal, North and South Blechhammer and made our second smash at Oswiecim today. The flak was very heavy and intense. Several planes were shot up fairly bad but made it back O.K. To make things worse the lead navigator was off the ball and took us over the Bratislava flak area. We were at 17,000 feet then and they really scared the daylights out of us. We picked up a nice flak hole in the windshield right in front of me. It threw plexi glass all over us but the piece of flak didn't have our number on it and went through the flight deck into the bomb bay without scratching any of us. It was too close for comfort though. Several planes really picked up some nice holes. A couple of the guys landed at Vis because of gasoline shortage or feathered engines. We really did a good job in knocking out the refinery. It was our first visual run in sometime.

Dec. 29, 1944

Sam got back today after attending the "Mickey" school at Bari for ten days. I will doubtless lose him now as he will be flying as a mickey operator in a radar ship from now on. With Ralph in the hospital with bronchitis for a couple of weeks I am pretty much alone as far as the officers on my crew are concerned. I'm afraid too that I may even lose, Mike, my engineer. He is 34 yrs. old and seems to be taking combat pretty hard. His nerves are bad and he is on edge most of the time. The flight surgeon told me today that he felt he would never make it through his tour unless he changed. The original boys are dropping out one by one. Eames was first to go when they took our bombardiers at Topeka; Seigel was next when I had him replaced the day we hit this squadron; Sam will be leaving us now to fly as a mickey man. If Ralph is checked out as a first pilot and Mike goes out on us there won't be much left of my original crew.

Jan. 31, 1945

After sitting around for over a month due to bad weather and an oversupply of crews to this squadron we finally got another mission. This one was to the oil refinery at Moosbierbaum. My copilot was Lt. Wynne and my navigator-bombardier Lt. Hassen. This was an ideal mission. No engine trouble, no surplus turns, and inaccurate flak. We flew Col. Keefer's wing in no. 3 spot for about the fourth time. It was a mickey run, but I believe we had our eggs right on the target. The mission was about the best all around mission I have been on. This was no. 13 for me.

Feb. 5, 1945

No. 14 today. This was Hassen's last one. Lt. Reynold's was my copilot.

We flew no. 4 spot today. Our box leader lost the formation temporarily and we had to pull excessive power for about an hour to catch them. It seemed that an unusual amount of engine trouble hit our box today. When we got back to the base there were only 3 of the original 7 ships left in our box. The other four all either turned back or else had to lag the formation after bombs away.

We hit the marshalling yards and oil storage facilities at Regensburg, Germany. Col. Snowden led the group.

February 13, 1945

Vienna Matzleinsdorf marshalling yards was our target today. This was our best mission I believe. It was executed perfectly as far as I am able to judge. We had a visual run on the target and the flak was heavy and intense, but no one was hit bad. We picked up three holes in our nose turret and nose navigator's section, but luckily the flak fragments missed connecting with anyone. John Oxler flew as navigator for me. Ralph flew as copilot for the first time in quite awhile. I cut the 15th notch today leaving 20 big ones yet to go. We plastered the target squarely this time.

February 18, 1945

Vienna Florisdorph Oil Refinery was our objective today but weather kept us from reaching it. We were on instruments part of the time as it was. Turned back about the time we passed over the Alps. The Air Force was in a generous mood though and gave us credit for the mission making 16 for me. Lt. Barnes was our navigator. As usual we flew no. 3 spot.

Vienna Central Marshalling Yds. made no. 17 for me today. This one took us right down main street on flak alley. No one was hit too badly though and we all got back to base. Lt. Cooper has been assigned to our crew as our permanent navigator. He flew his first one with us today.

No. 18 today. An abortive because of bad weather. We brought our bombs back to base.

Hit a bridge in the vital Brenner Pass today over which the Germans were trying to move troops from Italy to the Russian Front. This was 19 for me. We picked up a big flak hole right between Bill and I in the floor boards. Too close for comfort. Joe Herdman was shot down on this raid. We're hoping he is still alive even though it would mean he were a P.O.W.

Got no. 20 today. A good mission over the marshalling yards at Wienner Neustadt. Flew no. 4 spot for the fourth consecutive mission. Think we plastered the target

Going back to Dec. 18, 1944, my good friend Bob Sanderson ("Sandy") who was checking out a new crew crashed and was killed instantly at Ancona. He was hit badly over the target and tried to make it back to Ancona on two engines, but luck was against him. Sandy was a great boy and a fine pilot. I hated like everything to see him go.

Don Perry had to ditch in the Adriatic sometime ago after running out of gas. His engineer broke his pelvis and his radio operator broke his leg, but no one was killed. Don received the D.F.C.

March 14, 1945

I came back from my 21st mission today to learn that I was the dad of a baby girl. This is about the best news I ever hope to receive. Marian and Eleanor are both doing fine. Now I really have to get home.

The mission was to Brusk but we hit the marshalling yds. at Wiener Neustadt because the weather was better there. Flew no. 4 spot again. Major McCord led the group.

March 16, 1945

Amstteten, Austria marshalling yards was my 22nd target. Very smooth mission. We had a good percentage of our bombs on the target.

March 19, 1945

No. 23 today. A bombing mission run off at 17,000 feet on a no flak target. We hit the marshalling yards at Muhldorf, Germany. We are trying to cut off German supplies moving to the Russian front. Again we plastered the target squarely. Flew "The Dakota Queen" (279) today for the first time since it was flown back from the Ilse of Vis.

Sam Adams, my original navigator, has been missing in action since the Mar. 12th mission to Vienna. He was flying as a mickey man with Von Schriltz, a pilot from another sqdn. They were hit over the target and went down between the Russian and German lines. The Russians killed the nose navigator thinking they were Germans using an American B-24. Von Schriltz and his copilot are back but they do not know where the rest of the crew including Sam are. We hope they are still alive.

Joe Herdman's copilot returned from a partisan area near Pola where the crew bailed out after being hit on the Brenner Pass Raid of Feb. 28th. he says that Joe is probably a prisoner of war with several of the other fellows. One of them is beleived to have been killed by the Fascists as he hung in his chute coming down.

Neuberg air drome, north of Munich, was our target today. It is reported that we hit this target with as great a destructive accuracy as any airdrome hit in this war. It was a jet field housing the training program for Germany's new MC-262's. This was no. 24 for me.

Mar. 22, 1945

No. 25 today. An 8:40 haul to Kralupy oil Refinery, one of the last of Germanys oil refineries. Were almost hit by fighters today, but Jerry thought better when he saw our escort. For the third straight time we landed with more gas left than any other plane on the field.

Mar. 25

Hit Prague Tank works for no. 26 today. This is the first time Prague has been hit since the war began. We really initiated them right. Their gunners were rusty although they threw plenty of flak our way.

April 1, 1945

We bombed today from the lowest altitude yet - 14,000 feet. Our target was the Krieglach R.R. bridge near Graz. We could see the Russians advancing below us near the target. This was no. 27 for me. We leave for rest camp at Capri and Rome tomorrow.

April 11, 1945

Arrived back from Rome yesterday via a 454th plane. Flew no. 28 today when we hit a bridge in the Brenner Pass. Too much accurate flak to suit me. We didn't drop on the bridge however as it was smoke obscured from the banks of the preceeding group. We picked an alternate at Goito, Italy. Hit a big fuel dump there.

No. 29 today was something new for the heavies. We hit the front line area around Bologna. Quite a tactical operation. The 5th army boys laid down a barrage for us to tie up as much ack ack as possible, but Jerry still managed to make it plenty hot for us. We saw a lot of pink flak today. Looks like mountains of strawberry ice cream.

April 16, 1945

We tried to take another crack at Jerry's front line material today but the weather fooled us. The target was completely cloud covered so we had to bring our bombs back to base. We got credit for the mission, bombers - Giving me no. 30.

April 17, 1945

Today made three in a row for me. No. 31 - another crack at the Bologna area. The major really pulled a good piece of evasive action today. Only one ship was hit and he made it back to base O.K. We took a few light hits the 15th when we first hit Bologna but were untouched today.

April 18, 1945

Today made four in a row for me - all to the front lines in the Bologna area. The Fifth and Eighth Army's should begin to move any day now as we are leveling everything ahead of them. This no. 32 for me.

April 23, 1945

No 33 today. Hit a vital road bridge at Padua to cut off one of Jerries escape routes from northern Italy.

April 24, 1945

Hit an alternate target today - Ossoppo Motor Transport Depot. We went over the primary but didn't drop our bombs as the target was smoke obscured. This was 34 for me.

April 25, 1945

Well that last one is now behind me. It was my roughest mission. We hit the Linz Main Station. Our ship #34 was hit badly over the target. Tex took a flak hit in his left thigh. All our hydraulic lines were cut hopelessly so to land we had to crank our gear down manually, pump the flaps down, and then throw out parachutes to stop us when we were on the ground. We ended up at the end of the runway O.K. with no further damage to the plane or the fellows. We had well over 75 holes in our plane - some of which were amazingly close to some of us. In a way this was a good one to quit on because it made me more thankful than ever that I had finished.

May 8, 1945

The European war is over. Everyone is drunk but happy.

My last mission also proved to be the last one that the 15th Air Force flew. Guess I should consider myself lucky not to have missed that one even though it did scare the devil out of me.

Book design by Sam Cate-Gumpert

All photographs courtesy the Senator George McGovern Collection,
Dakota Wesleyan University Archives, Mitchell, South Dakota

Regular Sergeant

Staff Sergeant

First Sergeant

Chief Petty Off.

Petty Off. 1st Class

Petty Off. 2nd Class

Gen.

Air Corps and Flying Cadet

Military Intelligence

Inspector Gen.

1st Lieut. (silver)

Lieut. Col. (silver)

2nd Lieut. (gold)

Naval Avi

tion Observer's Badge

Milita

Chaplain (Jewisr

Chaplain (Christ.

Major (gold)

Electrician

Infantry

Quartermaste

Colonel

Storekeeper

Captain

Chaplain

Boatswain

s Badge

Signal Corps

Medical Corps

Carpenter's M.

Lieutenant

Lieut. Jr. Grade

Ensign

Cavalry

General Staff

Sanitary Reserves

Boatswain's M.

Admiral

Vice Admiral

Rear Admiral

Captain

Comman

Warfare

Nurses Corps

Gunner's M.

Aviation Mach. M.

Aviation Metalsmith

Aviation Ordnanceman

Av. Carpenter's M.

Cook

Aerograp

Av. Gen. Utility

inary

Technical Sergeant

Master Sergeant

Quartermaster

Radioman

Machinist M.